New Worlds

David Elliott

NEW WORLDS

Russian Art and Society 1900-1937

With 323 illustrations, in two colours throughout

Thames and Hudson

I should like to thank those who have been
of particular assistance in compiling this book:
John Bowlt, Gunn Brinson, Catherine Cooke, George
Costakis, Julia Elliott, Pamela Griffin, David King,
Alexander Lavrentiev,
State Mayakovsky Museum, Moscow,
Gordon McVay, John Milner, Angelica
Rudenstine, and the staff of Thames and Hudson.
Without their help the book would never have
seen the light of day.

Designed by David King   **Picture research by Alla Weaver**

Printed and bound in Spain
Artes Gráficas Toledo, S.A.
D.L. TO: 926 1986

Contents

Galvanizing the corpse

By 1900, a time of rapid industrialization and unprecedented social change, Russia was a country which had lost its soul. The old Empire, bolstered by an impassive autocracy, had begun to break up. The future was at best uncertain, at worst hopeless. A multitude of ideas, visions and theories were put forward about the nature of new world that inevitably and remorselessly would roll forward to take the place of the old. In 1904 Alexander Benois, critic, aesthete and painter, voiced these forebodings:

It is no longer the era of marquises. Within ten years or so the principles of the eighteenth century will have passed for ever. It is painful for me, the passionate champion of this affected art, to think about this; but I feel that the corpse can be galvanized no more. We are in need of a new life.

A bureaucratic, unwieldy, virtually medieval state, its backwardness justified by the divine authority of the Tsar, Russia had, until the middle of the last century, been a serfdom dominated by the anachronistic belief that social inequality had been ordained by God. Reform and liberalism of any kind were ruthlessly suppressed by censorship and the Okhrana, the tsarist secret police. The intelligentsia existed under sufferance and advanced political and social thinkers were either imprisoned or forced into exile.

Slowly the tide of liberal and nationalistic ideals which had engulfed the rest of Europe began to make itself felt: in March 1861 Tsar Alexander II liberated twenty-one million bonded serfs and made all such peasants free citizens with the right to own land. Such concessions, however, came too late and were not consistently maintained. The result was that, far from stemming the need and demand for a transformation of society, it was encouraged all the more. The first cracks in the ice of absolutism had begun to show; the whole apparatus of tsarist autocracy would soon be swept away in a raging and uncontainable flood.

Freed serfs left the land to work in growing industries in the towns. Here a cohesive and politically conscious working class was rapidly gaining strength. Fired by nationalistic fervour, populist intellectuals spread utopian socialist ideas among the peasants and, in the 1870s and 1880s, initiated a campaign of terrorism against tsarist officialdom. Secretly condemned to death by the terrorists in 1879 for failing to summon a Constituent Assembly, the once liberal Alexander II was finally assassinated in March 1881 by a bomb hurled by a young Polish student. Under the last two remaining Tsars, Alexander III and Nicholas II, repression and reaction became increasingly intense. It had become clear, however, by the end of the century, that the agent for political and social change would not be found in the peasant, backward and isolated in the vast steppes or *taiga* of provincial Russia, but among the increasingly politically active industrial workers in the major towns and cities in the west.

By 1937 the Soviet Union, as the Russian Empire

had then become, had been completely transformed economically, politically and socially, as a result of the deep-rooted desire for change which had swept away three centuries of Romanov rule in the October Revolution of 1917. This transformation was also directly attributable to the energy, ruthlessness and paranoia of Josef Stalin, the Communist Party Secretary who, since 1928, had increased his personal hold on the Party and had cut back the pluralism and experimentation of the early 1920s in favour of a monolithic party system. He achieved this fundamental change with an increasingly hardening autocracy; like the tsars before him, he maintained personal authority by relying on the secret police, the NKVD, and on institutionalized terror caused by the purges of opponents, real and imagined. Art was subordinated to the objectives of the Party and the Five Year Plan; a rigid orthodoxy was imposed on a culture which, from the early years of the twentieth century, had been remarkable in its diversity and energy. This energy, at times self-destructive, had led to a wide range of artistic styles, movements and tendencies in which artists, in a time of cultural and political ferment, had felt under pressure to clarify their aesthetics in line with their perceptions of social change. Some chose to bury their heads in the sand, some gleefully awaited destruction, others fought positively for a better life. Artists felt they had the freedom to predict the future as well as to reflect on what had already passed. In their aesthetic theories and views of the present and future, many artists crossed and recrossed the narrow dividing line between the visionary and the real.

This fundamental desire to transform reality can be seen at the root of both socialism and the movement towards modern art, the interests of the collective and the individual sometimes overlapping. The socialist and the modernist, of course, had their separate perspectives, their own visions of the kind of world they would like to see; for a few years after the Revolution, the two coincided with astounding results but there was always a fundamental tension between them. From the 1890s to the 1930s, 'socialist' art tended to be literal, figurative and populist while symbolism, an appreciation of primitive art and the arcane rationale of abstraction remained confined to the intelligentsia.

Art and reality

There were many inconsistencies and oppositions within the culture of pre-Revolutionary Russia. The most fundamental of these was the split between an idea of art which existed freely to be judged purely within its own terms, and a materialist, utilitarian theory which held that art should be didactic and in some sense illustrative of social, moral or political themes. This conflict continued through the cultural diversity of the 1920s to be finally reconciled in favour of the political and the didactic – what Andrei Zhdanov, Stalin's son-in-law and cultural boss, described in 1934 as the depiction of 'reality in its revolutionary development'. In the middle years of the last century enlightened writers such as Nikolai Chernyshevsky and Nikolai Dobrolyubov combined an awareness of national traditions with a sense of

Stasov and Gorky, 1904.

Church at Abramtsevo by Vasnetsov, 1880-2.

the artist's moral and social accountability. Such theories had a profound effect on many contemporary artists. In 1855 in his book *The Aesthetic Relations of Art and Reality,* Chernyshevsky set out his revolutionary creed: 'Art does not limit itself only to the beautiful . . . it embraces the whole of reality. . . . the content of Art is life in its social aspect.' In his novel *What is to be Done?,* written in 1864 in the cells of the St Peter-Paul fortress in Leningrad, Chernyshevsky gave flesh to his ideas of social revolution. In the 1890s and in the first decade of this century these ideas were avidly taken up by Lenin, who also appropriated Chernyshevsky's title for his 1902 pamphlet which transformed the organizational structure of the Revolutionary movement.

The most immediate direct influence of Chernyshevsky's theories, however, can be seen on the young group of painters who rebelled against the dead-handed classicism of the St Petersburg Academy to found, in 1870, the Society for Circulating Art Exhibitions. They soon became known as the Wanderers or *Peredvizhniki* in recognition of their efforts to make their work more widely available through travelling exhibitions and also in emulation of their own travels throughout Russia in search of a subject. Genre scenes showing social conditions were the most typical subjects of this group, which numbered among its most prominent members Ilya Repin, Vladimir Makovsky, Vassily Maximov, Nikolai Kasatkin and Abram Arkhipov, some of whom were still influential after the October Revolution. In Repin's words, their aim was to serve the highest aspects of life 'and to criticise mercilessly all the monstrosities of our vile reality'.

There was no shortage of patrons for this new art. From the 1870s Pavel Tretiakov had been intensively building his vast collection of Russian works of art, and in 1892 he gave it to the city of Moscow where it can still be seen today. Vladimir Stasov was an influential and articulate apologist in the Press. Savva Mamontov, the railway tycoon, provided board, working space and facilities for artist-craftsmen and musicians on his country estate at Abramtsevo, outside Moscow; he strongly encouraged a nationalist school in both art and opera. It was there, for example, that the artist Victor Vasnetsov first came into contact with the composer Rimsky-Korsakov, and they subsequently worked together designing sets and costumes for his operas. The Princess Tenisheva also established an artists' commune on her estate in Talashkino, near Smolensk, where the applied arts in a national style were given a new impetus.

By the turn of the century the positivist and scientific base of realism was under attack from the Symbolists but its vigour continued unabated. A second generation of painters such as Valentin Serov, Leonid Pasternak and Konstantin Korovin had absorbed the influence of French Impressionism and had begun to accommodate lighter colour and broken brushwork in their paintings. The writer Lev Tolstoy, although living in relative isolation on his country estate at Yasnaya Polyana, was still active and in 1897, in his long-awaited *What is Art?,* he added further fuel to Chernyshevsky's literary view by stressing the importance of art as a medium of communication: 'Great works of art are only great because they are accessible and comprehensible to everyone.'

In theatre as well, under the dominant influence

of Konstantin Stanislavsky at the new Moscow Arts Theatre, realism continued to flourish. At the opening of the theatre in June 1898 Stanislavsky put forward his democratic aims:

What we are undertaking is not a simple private affair but a social task. Never forget that we are striving to brighten the dark existence of the poor classes, to afford them minutes of happiness and aesthetic uplift, to relieve the gloom which envelopes them. Our aim is to create the first intelligent, moral, popular theatre, and to this end we are dedicating our lives.

Such ideals were clearly reflected in the early repertoire of the theatre; its sole backer, the industrialist Savva Morozov, was a strong supporter of the radical Social Democratic party and, with Gorky, was one of the sponsors of Lenin's radical journal *Vpered (Forward)*. Closely associated with Stanislavsky were Anton Chekhov, whose play *The Seagull* (1896) was given a triumphant revival in Moscow in 1898, and Maxim Gorky, whose first plays *The Lower Depths* and *The Philistines* were premièred in 1902. Chekhov's realism was spare and ironical; it focused on the moral paralysis of the Russian intelligentsia in the face of uncertainty and change. Gorky, eight years younger, went a step further and in Chekhov's own words was 'the first in Russia, and in the world at large, to have expressed contempt and loathing for the petty bourgeoisie. . . . he has done it at the precise moment when society is ready for protest.'

The Age of Silver 1893-1910

The social and political instability of these years was a fertile seedbed for experimental and innovatory art. As the rigid institutions of tsarist Russia were eroded, a new-found freedom began to flourish. Held back for so long, the tide of modern art and ideas swept across the country. Impressionism, Symbolism, Post-Impressionism, Fauvism and Cubism, movements which had been separated by generations in the West, were telescoped into little more than a decade. Symbolism and aestheticism found their earliest and most passionate supporter in Russia in the poet and critic Dmitri Merezhovsky, whose essay 'On Reasons for the Decline of Contemporary Russian Literature and On New Literary Trends' (1893) marked immense changes, not only in poetry and literature but throughout the arts; this remarkable flowering is now known as Russia's Silver Age.

The World of Art, a loose association of artists, literati, musicians and aesthetes based in St Petersburg, was one of the most influential groups. Formed in 1898 under the leadership of twenty-six-year-old Sergei Diaghilev, its central members included Leon Bakst, Alexander Benois, Dmitri Filosofov, Ivan Bilibin, Mtislav Dobuzhinsky, Dmitri Merezhovsky and Konstantin Somov. The group was important for the magazine it published and the exhibitions it organized and from the outset it was strongly identified with the first generation of Russian Symbolist poets, particularly Konstantin Balmont, Valery Briussov and Zinaida Gippius. Much depended on the discrimination and energy of Diaghilev, who galvanized the innate dilettantism of the group and

Benois, Nijinsky's costume in *Le Pavillon d'Armide*, 1907.

brought within its compass such diverse influences as the demonic Symbolist paintings of Mikhail Vrubel; the neo-nationalist pictures of Victor Vasnetsov; French Impressionism; ancient Russian icons and portraits; the seventeenth-century historicism of Benois; the starkly contrasted drawings of Aubrey Beardsley; the Nordic mythologies of the Finn, Axel Gallen-Kallela; and the Art Nouveau designs of Charles Rennie Mackintosh.

Of the exhibitions organized by the World of Art, the first and the last were the most important. The first opened in the Stieglitz Art Institute in St Petersburg in 1899 and showed over three hundred modern European works of art for the first time in Russia. Artists from both Moscow and St Petersburg were included along with the work of Monet, Degas, Puvis de Chavannes, Whistler and Böcklin; the work of the foreigners made a strong impact. The last World of Art exhibition held in 1906 took stock of the advances of modernism; it hinted at a new independence within Russian art, underlined the widening artistic rivalry between the 'Russian' dynamism of Moscow and the more conservative 'Western' taste of St Petersburg, and included large numbers of works by Victor Borisov-Musatov and Mikhail Vrubel. A sense of ethereality and dreaminess characterized this exhibition, looking forward to the Symbolist Blue Rose group which came together in Moscow in the following year.

The World of Art journal first appeared in 1898 and its most important role was as a disseminator of both national and Western art; for many Russian artists this magazine was the only available source of information on developments in the West. Diaghilev's ambitions for the journal were clear; he wrote that it should do no less than 'create a revolution in our artistic life'. Its production standards were high and the quality of the photogravure, typesetting and colour printing invited comparison with the best art magazines abroad. The costs of the journal were at first subsidized by the Princess Tenisheva and Savva Mamontov, but he had to back out in 1899 after his bankruptcy. Following arguments about policy with Diaghilev and Benois, the Princess withdrew her money in 1900 and the magazine was subsequently kept afloat by an annual grant of 10,000 roubles from the Tsar's private funds. The grant came to an end in 1904 as a direct result of the financial pressures of the Russo-Japanese War, but by that time the journal had been already weakened by internal dissension and it quickly folded. Encouraged by the ideal of the Wagnerian *Gesammtkunstwerk*, Scriabin's *Tone Poems* and the music of Rimsky-Korsakov, Diaghilev sought an inspired cross-fertilization between visual art, literature and music — a vision which was to find its apotheosis for him in exile in 1909 with the formation of the Ballets Russes.

Similar ideas were shared by the Symbolists who founded the Scorpion Publishing House in Moscow in 1899 with the specific aim of publishing new poetry and writing in a yearly almanac called *Northern Flowers;* in 1904 this was followed by *The Scales,* a periodical of Symbolist literature under the editorship of Valery Briussov.

A second wave of Symbolism in literature centred around Andrei Bely, Alexander Blok and Vyacheslav Ivanov, whose work, like that of the painters of the **9**

Blue Rose group, assumed a quasi-religious and mystical idealism. Ivanov synthesized the disparate sources of world religions into a personal mythology. For him the poet assumed a priest-like role and, rejecting the doctrine proposed by Briussov and his fellow Decadents of art as an end in itself, he looked back to the spiritual inspiration of Dostoevsky in a search for a higher truth which could be mediated through art. Bely, the most innovative of the three, modelled his prose poems – which he called 'symphonies' – on theories of musical composition, rather in the same way as the composer Alexander Scriabin related his compositions to colour theory, marking the score with colour notes and inventing a special colour/sound 'organ' to play them. Bely also experimented with the invention of new words and accelerated metres in the search for new structures and forms of expressing reality; this work was of great importance for the Futurist poets of the succeeding generation as well as for the Formalist writers and critics of the 1920s. The formal fragmentation of Bely's novels and poems was paralleled by his concern for the instability of modern society, which he depicted in a symbolic confrontation between East and West. Although dismissive of Briussov's salute to the impending apocalypse in poems such as *The Coming of the Huns* (1904-5) he nevertheless identified the spectre of advancing Asia, even closer after the Russo-Japanese War, with the cleansing forces of anarchy and chaos. 'History' to Bely 'was wind-eroded marl. The period of humanism had outlived its time and was over. A period of healthy barbarism was at hand.'

Other writers projected an apocalyptic vision of the future: Feodor Sologub's *Created Legend* (1914) and Sergei Belsky's *Under the Comet* (1910) looked forward to a time when a corrupt society would be destroyed by natural forces. In *Republic of the Southern Cross* (1907) Briussov looked forward to a socialist state at the South Pole nurtured under glass domes where, in spite of its logical structure, society perished as people had begun to act against their true desires.

This sense of disillusionment was also shared by Alexander Blok, the most lyrical of these poets. In his symbolic dramas, three of which were produced by Stanislavsky's protégé Vsevolod Meyerhold in St Petersburg between 1906 and 1908, a mood of self-doubt emerged. Finished in the early days of 1906, *The Fairground Booth,* in which Meyerhold himself took the lead role of Pierrot, accurately captured the mood of the dislocated Russian intelligentsia after the 1905 Revolution, in which ambivalence was elevated above truth, irony above sincerity and impassivity above love. This language of opposites, an early form of theatrical alienation, gave Symbolism a new dimension. The work was difficult to understand and created a *succès de scandale;* Ivanov and the other Symbolists condemned Blok for presenting an image of a spiritually exhausted world, while the audience, accustomed by the realist plays of Stanislavsky to identify with the characters on stage, became confused when calculated grotesquerie demanded that they judge and evaluate their own reactions. When the 1917 Revolution came, however, Blok welcomed it. In the religious symbolism of his poem *The Twelve,* written in a trance early in 1918, the Revolution became mystically trans-

Brlussov, 1910.

Bakst, *Portralt of Andrel Bely,* 1905.

formed by the casual death of a young girl at the hands of Red Guards; this implied that redemption and a new truth could be found through the atonement of blood.

Among younger writers a reaction soon set in against the mysticism and apocalyptic excess of the Symbolists. In 1912 Nikolai Gumilov, the self-proclaimed leader of the 'Acme' group – as they were contemptuously described by Bely – published a manifesto in *Apollo* which called for the expression of a palpable and visible reality with unambiguous concrete imagery and simple language. The other main advocates of Acmeism were Anna Akhmatova, who was married to Gumilov, and Osip Mandelstam.

In painting, the Symbolist aesthetic can be seen in the work of the Blue Rose group as well as in the more robustly coloured work of Kuzma Petrov-Vodkin. The Blue Rose artists – Victor Borisov-Musatov, Pavel Kuznetsov and Martiros Saryan – were taken up by Nikolai Ryabushinsky's magazine *The Golden Fleece* whose first issue (1906) was dedicated to Mikhail Vrubel and Victor Borisov-Musatov. Published in emulation of the work of the World of Art, its articles tended towards the mystical and spiritual, lacking the analytical and scholarly emphasis of its predecessor. In a preface to the first edition, Ryabushinsky spoke up for the supremacy of a transcendent view in a world where bloody conflict had just made itself too uncomfortably felt:

We embark on our path at a formidable time. Around us, like a raging whirlpool, seethes the rebirth of life. In the thunder of the fight, amid the urgent questions raised by our time, amid the bloody answers provided by our Russian reality, the eternal for many fades and passes away. . . . Art is eternal for it is founded on the unchanging. . . . Art is whole for its single source is the soul. Art is symbolic for it bears within it the symbol. . . . Art is free for it is created by the free impulse of creation.

In 1908 Ryabushinsky organized the Salon of the Golden Fleece, an exhibition which included the young Russian painters Mikhail Larionov and Natalia Goncharova as well as a section of 197 modern French paintings, which incorporated work by Van Gogh, Cézanne, Matisse and Gauguin. There was a strong contrast between the work of the Russians, which in mood hearkened back to the wistfulness of Puvis de Chavannes or to the muted decorative ambience of Les Nabis, and the bright French paintings here seen publicly in Russia for the first time. It was their primitive energy and pictorial sophistication rather than the tired colour harmonies of the Blue Rose which gave the next generation of young Russian painters an impetus.

The last days of the Empire

Within two years from the beginning of 1903 political stability throughout the whole of Russia had deteriorated rapidly. In the south a wave of strikes started in Rostov-on-Don and spread to Baku and Odessa; workers were massacred by tsarist troops and the strikes spread to St Petersburg. In February 1904 Russia engaged in the futile and disastrous war with

Annenkov, illustration for Blok's *The Twelve*, 1920.

Bilibin, caricature of the Emperor, 1905.

Japan which resulted in the loss of Port Arthur and a humiliating defeat. In August, the Minister of the Interior was assassinated. The Tsar, increasingly out of touch with his people, had given his blessing to the Orthodox and quasi-military Union of the Russian People which sponsored groups of thugs, the Black Hundreds, to organize pogroms against the Jews. His wife, the Tsarina Alexandra, was similarly authoritarian, stoutly maintaining that 'the Russians love to be caressed by the horsewhip'. On 9 January 1905 when 150,000 marched on the Winter Palace in St Petersburg to present a petition to the Tsar asking for reforms, the reaction was predictable. The troops opened fire: over 200 demonstrators were killed and another 2000 wounded. This barbaric act provoked worldwide condemnation as well as mutiny and insubordination throughout the country. In October a general strike was called and in response, under duress, the Tsar was forced to concede a Constitutional Manifesto recognizing basic civil liberties and creating the State Duma, a parliament and legislative assembly. Maxim Gorky's attitude to the Revolution of 1905 was uncompromising: he regarded it as 'a chance to destroy the stupid gluttons and syphilitics who have ruined and shamed Russia'. Many other artists joined in the revolt and, for the short period when the censorship laws were relaxed, a spate of viciously satirical anti-establishment magazines flooded off the presses. Once the moment of revolution had passed, however, these were suppressed as it became clear that the Tsar had no intention of instituting any real reform. Gorky, a spiritual and financial supporter of Lenin's Bolsheviks, was forced to leave the country and he was able to return only in 1913 after a political amnesty had been declared.

Artists of many different persuasions rallied to the Revolution. 'Bloody Sunday', as the massacre of peaceful demonstrators became known, was an event of such horror that, for a time, the bourgeois intelligentsia and workers were united in their condemnation. For one magazine in 1906 Boris Kustodiev, a realist painter and pupil of Ilya Repin, created the memorable image of the figure of Death, a bloodstained skeleton, stalking the barricades; it was an image he revived and turned on its head fifteen years later in *The Bolshevik*, a large oil painting in which the figure of Death has been replaced by the robust form of the new worker – saviour of the Russian people.

Artists of more modernist tendencies also participated in direct criticism of the régime. A number of these – Mtislav Dobuzhinsky, Evgeny Lanceray, Konstantin Somov, and Ivan Bilibin – were associated with Sergei Diaghilev's World of Art group. They became affiliated to the new Constitutional Democratic (Kadet) Party and contributed satirical drawings to the new magazines. In 1905, Dobuzhinsky, with Lanceray, Somov and Alexander Benois as co-signatories, published his manifesto *The Voice of Artists* simultaneously in three St Petersburg newspapers: 'beauty will be abolished and forgotten in the mighty wave of urgent practical needs,' he proclaimed. 'In constructing the new life, artists must contribute to the common cause but not only as citizens. . . . Artists are confronted with the task to decorate this new unknown life. . . . Our appeal must be for . . . the masses to be educated in the spirit of beauty.' Hardly a panacea for the practical problems which faced Russia, such utopian solutions

Kuznetsov, *The Blue Fountain*, 1905.

Massacre of Jews, Odessa 1905.

Kustodiev, 'Death Stalks the Streets', 1906.

Kustodiev, *The Bolshevik*, 1921.

reflected their essentially middle-class background and echoed the spirit of the slogan 'Art is free, life is paralysed' which had appeared in the books and magazines produced by Diaghilev.

In the aftermath of 1905 there was a polarization between those who sought spiritual withdrawal into an idealist utopia and those who were overcome by a pervasive sense of hopelessness and depression. Suicides among the intelligentsia increased: prevented by his family in 1905 from radically improving conditions for the workers in his factories Savva Morozov, Stanislavsky's patron, blew his brains out; in the same year Sergei Sergeievich, the youngest son of the art collector Sergei Shchukin, threw himself into the Moscow river and was drowned. This sense of nihilism found further expression in a cult of extremes. The plays of Strindberg and Wedekind, which focused on problems of sexuality, now appeared in Russian translation. Gothic horror, neurosis, pathological sex and madness were the stock in trade of the plays and short stories of Leonid Andreev, and the novel *Sanin* (1907) by Mikhail Artsybashev took the view that conventional morality had become outmoded and proposed unlimited and exploitative sexual license in its place. *Sanin* took St Petersburg by storm, and its message of free love was perverted by groups of men who, in 'Saninist' sex clubs, fantasized that they had inherited the nihilist traditions of the 1860s. The feeling of moral decay spread: a flood of pornographic books appeared, some illustrated by members of the World of Art; rumours began to circulate about the Court and the relationship between the Tsarina and Gregory Rasputin, the peasant mystic monk who exerted a hypnotic power of healing over the haemophilia of the Tsarevich Alexei. Rasputin's drunkenness and sexual incontinence were already common knowledge and undermined confidence in the sanity of the German-born Tsarina.

When the Duma was recalled in 1912, the opposition, fuelled by the increasingly remote life of the tsarist court, maintained its continuous but impotent criticism of State policy. This was given a brief respite in 1914 by Russia's entry into the war with Germany, which was accompanied by an upsurge of popular patriotism. But as defeat followed defeat, food shortages became acute and inflation eroded the savings of the middle classes, widespread criticism of the Tsar's incompetence increased. To many, removal of the Tsar seemed to be the only way to win the war and to protect the future of the Empire.

By February 1917 bread riots in Petrograd* had precipitated open revolt; the pressure for change could no longer be contained and the house of the Romanovs was toppled by the bourgeois 'Revolution' of the liberal Provisional Government. In April Lenin and a number of other Bolshevik Revolutionaries, aided by the Germans, returned to Russia from exile. Alexander Kerensky, Minister for War and leader of the Provisional Government, was determined to bring about a reversal in Russian fortunes in the war but he fatally misjudged the mood of the people. By the time he realized that the majority wanted peace, all popular support for his government had evaporated. Troops returning from the front supported the peace plans of the Bolsheviks and swelled their numbers until by September there were Bolshevik majorities in both the Moscow and Petrograd Soviets.

Malevich, anti-German poster, c. 1915.

Kerensky, 1917.

*St Petersburg was renamed Petrograd in 1914 and, after the death of Lenin in 1924, it became known as Leningrad.

Leon Trotsky, President of the Petrograd Soviet, engineered the final takeover; on 24 October the Petrograd garrison acknowledged the Soviet as sole authority, to be followed, on the next day, by the troops at the St Peter-Paul Fortress; the Winter Palace was stormed that night and the troops still loyal to the Provisional Government refused to use force in its defence. In the reverberating echoes of Lenin's slogan 'Peace, Bread and Land', the poor at last had found their voice. Exhausted and debilitated, the Empire and the social order which supported it were swept away – six Red Guards died in the struggle. In a few hours the coup, which was to become known as the October Revolution, was complete.

One of the first acts of the new Bolshevik government was the decree of peace with Germany, dated 26 October; by December an Armistice had been declared and the peace was formalized at Brest-Litovsk on 3 March 1918.

By the summer of 1918, however, Counter-Revolutionary (White) forces had mobilized and in August Lenin was seriously injured when an attempt was made on his life. After this, the Bolsheviks took complete command and wrested by force the last vestiges of political power from the rival Socialist Revolutionaries. The Civil War between the Reds and the Whites continued from December 1917 to November 1920.

New beginnings 1910-21

A search for the primitive, the heartbeat of ancient Russia, and a mystical yearning to express the spirit of the countryside inspired young avant-garde painters such as Goncharova, Larionov, Marc Chagall, David Burliuk and Kasimir Malevich; they looked to the simple life of the peasant, to the rough woodblock broadsheet (*lubok*) and to the shop signs and paintings of the Georgian naive painter Niko Pirosmani – discoveries which gave them a new vocabulary of images. Such influences, together with an intimate knowledge of the latest developments in Parisian painting, culled from the Moscow collections of Ivan Morozov and Sergei Shchukin, gave these artists the courage to experiment while, at the same time, retaining a sense of their specifically Russian identity.

There was, however, another more cautious tendency within the avant-garde and by 1910 two opposing factions could be clearly identified in the Knave of Diamonds – the leading exhibition group: the 'Russians', led by Larionov, and the 'French', led by the more conservative painter Aristarkh Lentulov. The following year a split was provoked when the 'primitive' Russians left to form The Donkey's Tail – named by Larionov in delight after the story of the artist who had tied a paintbrush to a donkey's tail and had successfully submitted the resulting canvas to the Paris Salon des Indépendants. Against this attack, the Knave of Diamonds maintained its dignity, seriousness and strong orientation towards French painting. Its leading members were Robert Falk, Pyotr Konchalovsky, Alexander Kuprin and Ilya Mashkov. These artists adopted the analytical and structural method of Cubism but were not able to move from this to complete abstraction.

From 1910 to 1917 the avant-garde in both St

Larionov, *Portrait of Vladimir Tatlin*, c. 1911.

Petersburg/Petrograd and Moscow was in ferment. In manifestos, cabarets, groups and counter-groups, young artists struggled to express a new energy and vitality against the darkening twilight of the decaying Empire. Both Goncharova and Larionov, for a time the pace-setters in this rapid period of change, embraced the challenge to civilization so feared by Briussov and Bely by seeking regeneration in the art and mystical energy of the East. 'For me,' Goncharova wrote in 1913, 'the East means the creation of new forms, and the extension and deepening of the problems of colour. This will help me to express modern life – its living beauty – better and more vividly. . . . I aspire towards a sense of nationality and the East, not to confine my art but, on the contrary, to make it all-embracing and universal . . . .' For Larionov the search for the primitive, crudely expressed and therefore more direct and honest in feeling, was his first step towards a new kind of painting which did not have to be dominated by the demands of representation.

After The Donkey's Tail, subsequent exhibitions organized by Larionov included The Target (1913) and No. 4 (1914); in retrospect, these exhibitions can be seen to be of seminal importance – at the time they provided important outlets for radical work by many young artists. The Target incorporated the first major showing of Larionov's and Goncharova's new Rayonist paintings, which crossed the borderline between the figurative and abstract. While not of lasting influence on other artists, these works were an important development of what Larionov called 'self-sufficient' painting and as such were valuable in clearing the ground for younger artists. Larionov was committed to the development of art which was founded on a visual and perceptive rather than on a literary, moral or mystical base:

Rayonism erases the barriers that exist between a picture's surface and nature . . . . The objects that we see in life play no role here but that which is the essence of painting itself can be shown here best of all – the combination of colour, its saturation, the relationship of coloured masses, depth, texture . . . it imparts a sensation of the extra-temporal – of the spatial; in it we can perceive the sensation of the fourth dimension.

A concern for the pictorial representation of the fourth dimension was at the root of much new non-figurative painting. Larionov as well as Malevich, Vladimir Tatlin, and the Futurist poet Velimir Khlebnikov, were all influenced by Pyotr Uspensky's philosophical text *Tertium Organum. Key to the Laws of the Universe* (1911). The fourth dimension was both a reality and an ideal to which man could progress; the flavour and attraction of Uspensky's ideas can be sensed in this extract from the book:

The immediate future of our race is indescribably hopeful. There are, at present, three impending revolutions: 1 – the material, economic and social revolution which will depend upon and result from the establishment of aerial navigation; 2 – the economic and social revolution which will abolish individual ownership and rid the earth at once of two immense evils – riches and poverty; 3 – the psychic revolution.

Group of Petrograd Futurists in Kulbin's studio, 1915. *Standing:* **Mayakovsky;** *seated:* **Kulbin, Rozanova, Lourié and Kamensky.**

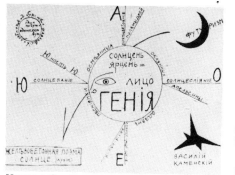

Kamensky, ferro-concrete poem, c. 1913.

Larionov's abrasive character and desire to break down dead convention also undoubtedly had a strong effect on the younger Russian Futurists. Acting in a Futurist film, *Drama in Cabaret 13* (1914), now lost, Larionov appears carrying the half-naked body of Goncharova in his arms; both their faces are painted with symbols. In the same year the Italian Futurist F.T. Marinetti made his first visit to Russia. Marinetti's *Futurist Manifesto,* an exhortation that the arts should express the violence of change in an industrial world, had been published in Russia in 1909. It had a profound influence and within a short period had been digested and recast into a specifically Russian form. During 1912 and 1913 both the Rayonists and Futurists, including David Burliuk and Vladimir Mayakovsky, had scandalized the public by making a number of appearances with painted faces. When asked by a St Petersburg magazine to explain his action, Larionov answered, 'We have joined art to life. After the long isolation of the artist we have loudly summoned life and life has invaded art, it is time for art to invade life. The painting of our faces is the beginning of the invasion.'

Other avant-garde tendencies at this time included the St Petersburg Impressionists or 'intuitivists', supported by the 'mad army doctor' painter Nikolai Kulbin and composer-artist Mikhail Matiushin, and the Union of Youth Movement which at first shared many of the Symbolist ideas of the Blue Rose group but which, by 1912, had gravitated towards the ideas of the Futurists. In St Petersburg, Futurism coalesced round the Ego-Futurism of Igor Severyanin, the free-wheeling ambience of the Stray Dog Café and the music of Arthur Lourié; in Moscow the Hylea group, subsequently called the Cubo-Futurists, rallied round poet-painter David Burliuk and the poets Velimir Khlebnikov, Vladimir Kamensky (an aviator), Alexei Kruchonykh and Vladimir Mayakovsky. The 'hooligan artists' of Hylea, all of provincial origin, soon became the symbol of a generation in revolt – dressed as dandies, they walked through the centre of Moscow cat-calling at passers-by and they insulted audiences and provoked fights at the concerts they gave. In 1913 they adopted for their manifesto the inflammatory title *A Slap in the Face of Public Taste:* 'We alone are the image of our time,' they cried. 'The past is narrow. The Academy and Pushkin – less intelligible than hieroglyphics. Pushkin, Dostoevsky, Tolstoy and the rest of them should be thrown overboard from the steamer of the present time.'

Alongside the iconoclastic destruction of the old, a concern with the structure of the new art, visual and literary, lay at the root of Futurism. In his diagrammatic 'ferro-concrete poems', Kamensky combined the two, as did Khlebnikov in verses in which words were dislocated from their meanings and phrases were repeated to build a picture of sound. In doing this he invented a new concept, that of *zaum* or trans-sense – a system of communication which would cross the boundaries of conventional words to establish a universal language which could be intuitively understood. Small private presses produced many artists' books, overturning all previous conventions of fine printing in memorable combinations of image, texture and verse.

Futurism also made a strong impact on theatre. The autobiographical play *Vladimir Mayakovsky: A*

Kruchonykh, Malevich and Matiushin in Uusikirkko, 1913.

Tragedy was written and performed by its protagonist early in 1914, and the opera *Victory over the Sun* was written by Kruchonykh with a prologue by Khlebnikov in 1913; the music was by Matiushin and costumes and sets were designed by Malevich. Both plays were examples of the 'theatre of the future man' which had been given this grand title at the First All-Russian Congress of Singers of the Future (attended by Malevich and Kruchonykh) in July 1913, at Matiushin's dacha at Uusikirkko. For Aristarkh Lentulov, who designed the sets for Mayakovsky's play, the poet seemed to be expressing 'utopian realism, a kind of dream of the new life'. The theme of *Victory over the Sun* was similar: in Matiushin's words, it was the 'Victory over the old, accepted concept of the beautiful sun . . . over romanticism and empty verbosity.' The unforgettable image of the black square ran throughout the performance as a leitmotif with many forms and meanings: above all, it was a symbol of the defeat of the sun; it was also a decoration on the costume of the man who dug the sun's grave – a black hole; it was a schematic end view of the coffin in which the corpse of the sun had been interred, as well as a symbol of the victory of the new order. At the climactic point its image dominated the stage as a gigantic painted backcloth.

During 1915 three major exhibitions of avant-garde art took place: Tramway V opened in Petrograd in March and was subtitled The First Exhibition of Futurist Painting; the Exhibition of Painting 1915 opened in Moscow in April; and, at the end of the year, 0.10 The Last Futurist Exhibition opened in Petrograd. In the course of these exhibitions the leadership of the avant-garde moved away from Larionov, Goncharova and the Futurists towards two opposing tendencies: the metaphysical idealists, led by Malevich, and the materialists, who gravitated towards Tatlin. At 0.10 Malevich showed his latest 'Suprematist' paintings – flat, brightly coloured geometric forms floating on the liberated space of a white ground with such titles as *Pictorial Realism of a Footballer* and *Colour Masses in the Fourth Dimension*. Malevich had first used the term 'Suprematist' in relation to his work as early as September 1914; for him it embodied the supreme or ultimate which could only be attained once the jaded representations of previous art had been buried. The titles of the works reflected his belief that painting was a transcendent activity through which a fourth dimension or even life beyond death could be represented; these ideas were developed in his pamphlet *From Cubism to Suprematism,* which was privately published in three editions in Moscow during 1915 and 1916. This metaphysical approach was in stark contrast to that of Tatlin, his rival, whose corner-mounted counter-reliefs so evidently took as their subject the disparate materials of which they were made. These divisions became even more clear in a subsequent exhibition, The Store, organized in 1916, in vacant shop premises on Moscow's Kuznetsky Most; factions had now formed round each artist. This was the last major exhibition of avant-garde art before the Revolution.

Malevich began to experiment with forms which he developed into a cosmic architecture – a system of balance and harmony which could serve and decorate the new Revolutionary order. From 1916 the flat colour areas in his paintings had begun to take on

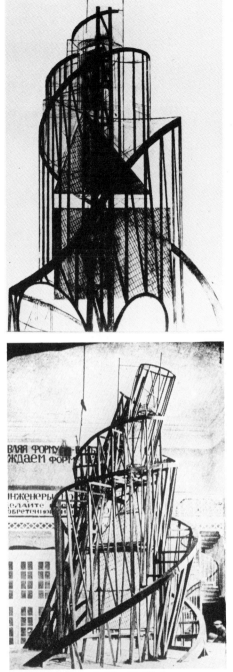

Design and model for Tatlin's Monument to the Third International, 1919.

a three-dimensional aspect, a tendency which became more strongly pronounced when in 1919, at the invitation of Chagall, head of the new Vitebsk Free Art Workshops, he travelled to Vitebsk to teach. A charismatic and radical figure, Malevich gathered an enthusiastic band of young supporters in the Workshops. His slogan, 'Integrate Suprematism into Life', provided a rallying point for all progressive staff and students. With the taste for acronyms which became such a strong characteristic of the new Soviet state, the Malevich faction was called Unovis (the Champions of the New Art). Their symbol, a black square sewn on the sleeves of their garments, testified their allegiance to the tenets of Suprematism and revolution in art. While at Vitebsk Malevich worked closely with Lazar (El) Lissitzky, an architect turned painter who ran the print workshop at the art school. Separately they began to work on utopian schemes and blueprints for future world development. Lissitzky's drawings and paintings of floating three-dimensional space-age structures were given the generic title of *Prouns* (projects for the affirmation of the new); he described them as plans 'for the new Communist cities of the future'. Malevich's architectural schemes appeared later in the 1920s.

Futurism also played a vital part in the evolution of Tatlin's work after the Revolution, although the lessons he learned from it were of a practical and formal nature which related more to questions of material and structure. These were clearly embodied in his masterwork – the design for the Monument to the Third International (1919) in which for the first time, the engineering forms of Constructivism were combined with social commitment. The Monument was planned as a massive structure which would straddle the banks of the River Neva in Petrograd. It was designed to function as and symbolize the executive core of the Workers' International – the nerve-centre from which the inevitable spread of world Communism would be governed. Consisting of two concentric conical spirals with a cylinder emerging from the head, the structure was hung on the dynamic forward thrust of a backbone girder. The design embodied the social organization of the new Communist world state and its spiral form was chosen to embody the concept of cyclical dialectic.

Following Khlebnikov's theories of human activity evolving through time in harmony with the sun, stars and space, the three rotating levels within the tower each fulfilled a separate function. On the first floor a cube, which rotated once every year, would house the full meetings of the International; at the second level, a pyramid, rotating once every month, would accommodate the executive and administrative committees; at the third and top level a cylindrical, or in some plans a hemispherical, room would provide the communications centre for the dissemination of the decisions of the International – this incorporated a telegraph office, a radio station, a printing press and a large external screen for projecting information. In 1919, however, the prospect of world Communism was far from immediate as the new Soviet state was fighting for its survival in a bloody civil war.

Before the Revolution, the Bolsheviks had paid relatively little thought to the way in which they would administer the country once they had taken power. In the early days after October 1917 many pragmatic decisions had to be taken: in education, art, industry, **15**

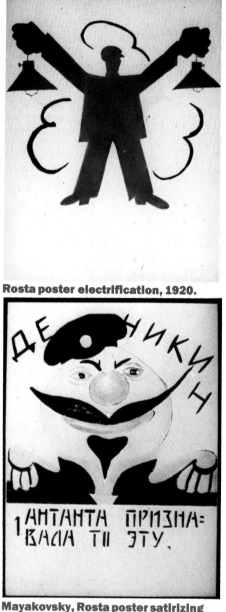

Rosta poster electrification, 1920.

Mayakovsky, Rosta poster satirizing General Denikin, 1919.

'The Red Ploughman', Bolshevik poster, c. 1921.

indeed throughout the whole economy, responsibility was devolved onto local activist groups, or cadres, which, it was hoped, would act on Party decrees and transform the old hierarchical institutions of the Empire into new democratic organizations. There was no set pattern and in many cases efforts were made to retain specialists in jobs they held before the Revolution; yet in the arts the restructuring opened many possibilities for the production of new work which embodied Revolutionary ideals. One of the most important policies of the new administration was to ensure free access and exhibition in the streets, theatres, clubs and museums. Anatoly Lunacharsky, intellectual, writer, critic, co-editor of the literary journal *New World* and, most significantly, head of the new People's Commissariat for Public Enlightenment (Narkompros), played a critical role in commissioning and funding a wide variety of cultural activities from 1918 to his involuntary retirement in 1929. In the period immediately after the Revolution, he set out a deliberately pluralistic policy by sponsoring the Futurists as well as most traditional artists, and by publishing their short-lived newspaper *The Art of the Commune*.

In 1919 Gosizdat, the state publishing house, was set up, and throughout the 1920s Maxim Gorky's publishing house Vsermirnaia (Universal) and the magazine *Red Virgin Soil*, edited by Alexander Voronsky, provided a platform for intellectuals who were not directly affiliated to the Party. A number of these writers, including Vsevolod Ivanov, Konstantin Fedin, Mikhail Zoshchenko and Evgeny Zamyatin, were all members of the Serapion Brotherhood which, during the 1920s, espoused the cause of extreme individualism in literature, oblivious to outside direction.

At the opening of the State Free Workshops in the former Petrograd Academy of Arts in October 1918, Lunacharsky set out his faith in the vitality of a new Revolutionary art, echoing Mayakovsky's famous slogan: 'Let us make the squares our palettes, the streets our brushes!' He urged: 'despite our impoverishment . . . we are on the way to a flowering of the arts . . . a new art has arisen to change the appearance of the towns as quickly as possible, to express the new life in works of art, to get rid of that mass of sentiment which is obnoxious to the people, to create new forms of public buildings and monuments.' Ephemeral agitational art (agit-prop) sprang up on the streets: large cartoon-like posters proclaimed to the barely literate the need for vigilance against counter-revolution as well as the social benefits of the new state and its public health programmes against disease and famine. Monuments to Revolutionary heroes such as Danton, Bakunin, Robespierre, Marx and Engels were quickly made and exhibited in the squares and public spaces. Young groups of actors wrote and performed simple political sketches at public gatherings and for Red Army troops at the front in the Civil War. Through the IZO (Fine Arts Section) of Narkompros, avant-garde artists such as Olga Rozanova, Alexander Rodchenko and Varvara Stepanova were involved in the establishment of the new museums of contemporary art, in the regeneration of craft industries and in the organization of broadly based State Exhibitions.

But there was no consensus on the path that lay ahead: the work shown in the Tenth State Exhibition,

Mayakovsky, poster advertising the free health service, mid 1920s.

Pashkov, poster against spitting, mid 1920s.

Poster advertising 'Blue Blouse' performances – groups of young actors who perform agit plays, mid 1920s.

subtitled Non-Objective Creation and Suprematism, held in Moscow in 1919, most clearly highlighted the conflicting points of view between the older and younger generations of the avant-garde. On one side, the forty-one-year-old Malevich exhibited his *White on White* paintings, works about which he wrote in the catalogue: 'I have broken the boundary of colour limits and come out into white. . . . Swim! the free white sea of infinity lies before you.' The *Black on Black* paintings of Rodchenko, thirteen years younger and an admirer of Tatlin, however, punctured Malevich's idealist bubble: 'as a basis for my work I put nothing.' Rodchenko was set on a path which transcended all questions of styles and 'isms'; this was to be 'the beginning of my resurrection. With the funeral bells of colour painting, the last "ism" was accompanied to its grave, the last lingering hopes of love are destroyed and I leave the house of dead truths. Analysis, not synthesis, is creation. . . .' In an ironic side swipe at Malevich he added, 'Christopher Columbus was neither a writer nor a philosopher, he was merely the discoverer of new countries.'

From this time Rodchenko's work was based increasingly on the exploration of the language of visual representation through an examination of the properties of colour, line and repeated structural element in two or three dimensions. By 1921, in an exhibition laconically called 5 × 5 = 25, Rodchenko, with fellow artists Liubov Popova, Alexander Vesnin, Varvara Stepanova and Alexandra Exter, had reached the logical extreme of his experiments and he declared that the last picture had been painted. In this exhibition Rodchenko exhibited three monochrome canvases, of red, yellow and blue, the last paintings he was to produce until the late 1930s. Henceforth the artist should work not out of inner compulsion but out of a feeling of social responsibility. Art would be replaced by construction, as 'construction represents the contemporary demand for organization and the utilitarian use of materials'. Most of these artists had been members of Inkhuk (the Institute of Artistic Culture) which for eighteen months from the spring of 1920, as part of Narkompros, had been at the forefront of avant-garde aesthetic debates in Moscow. The first director of Inkhuk was Vassily Kandinsky, who encouraged a synthetic and psychological analysis of artistic problems. However, by the autumn of 1921 he had resigned to return to Germany and the Institute had become identified with the Production Art movement which advocated the supremacy of applied art and industrial design as a true reflection of the Communist ideal.

Unsentimental, scientific and logical, Constructivism had broken away from an obsession with 'the culture of material' – an analysis of the material properties of art – towards a concern with production in industry. Artists were encouraged to work as designers in factories. In 1921, in his book *From the Easel to the Machine,* the critic Nikolai Tarabukin put forward three ideas in support of production art, and in 1922 the designer and polemicist Alexei Gan, in a book simply titled *Constructivism,* announced the death of conventional art, looking forward to the millennium of the Marxist future: 'Art arose naturally, developed naturally and disappeared naturally. MARXISTS MUST WORK IN ORDER TO ELUCIDATE ITS DEATH SCIENTIFICALLY AND TO FORMULATE NEW

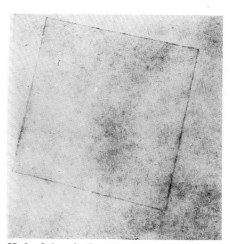

Malevich painting, *White on White,* 1917-18.

Rodchenko painting, *Black on Black,* 1918.

PHENOMENA OF ARTISTIC LABOUR WITHIN THE NEW HISTORIC ENVIRONMENT OF OUR TIME.'

The destruction of the old art had been one of the main aims of the Futurists before the Revolution and this had been quickly adopted by the Constructivists during the early 1920s. There was also a Marxist justification for this view as articulated in the writings of Alexander Bogdanov, a novelist, medical doctor and Revolutionary of 1905, who was the leading theorist of Proletkult (Proletarian Culture). Bogdanov maintained that art before the Revolution was inevitably imbued with the hierarchical values of tsarism and therefore diametrically opposed to the new order. As a first step towards the creation of a truly proletarian culture, he felt that the art of the past should be restricted and in some cases actively suppressed; some of his supporters were rather too zealous in translating words into action and embarked on a campaign of active iconoclasm. This quickly earned the disapproval of both Lenin and Lunacharsky who were concerned to preserve the artefacts and diverse traditions of pre-Revolutionary culture, as neither wished to alienate the intelligentsia and 'fellow-travellers' whom they regarded as an essential element in the construction of a new Communist state. As a result in 1920 the independence of Proletkult was revoked by a decree of the Central Committee of the Russian Communist Party and it was made subordinate to Lunacharsky's Commissariat for Public Enlightenment.

Men and machines

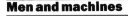

More positively, as its name suggests, Proletkult was engaged in the creation and encouragement of new literary and cultural cadres from the ranks of the workers. It was organized on urban, district and factory levels and ran *litstudios* – literary workshops – as well as special sections devoted to painting, theatre and music. Bogdanov's view that 'Art was the most powerful weapon for the organization of collective forces' was reflected in the Proletkult publishing programme, which produced over twenty journals. Proletkult also argued for a completely new basis to Communist life. Young girls would be forbidden to keep dolls; new forms of collective sport would be developed and new personal names invented which reflected the priorities and values of socialism.

Technology, the relationship between the individual and the collective, the 'mystery' of labour and the belief in a 'cosmic' future were central themes in Proletkult literature. Alexei Gastev was one of the most influential of its poets and his most popular anthology *Shockwork Poetry* (1918) included poems with titles like 'Factory Whistles, Rails and Tower' – a precursor and literary equivalent of the Symphony of Labour performed in November 1922 by soldiers and workers in Baku using factory sirens, cannons and aircraft engines as instruments.

Gastev was particularly fascinated by robotics and the time and motion studies of the American cybernetician Frederick W. Taylor, and he allied these to theories of human psychology. In 1919 he wrote chillingly of the 'mechanization, not only of gestures, not only of production methods, but of everyday thinking, coupled with extreme rationality [which]

'The Red Star', from amateur performance, 1926.

Gastev, c. 1919.

normalizes to a striking degree the psychology of the proletariat.' Lunacharsky could see the sinister implication of these ideas, describing them as 'heralding an epoch of pure technology' and introducing 'the idea of subordinating people to mechanisms and of the mechanization of man'. For Gastev this concern became an all-consuming passion and he was subsequently made Director of the Central Institute of Labour (TsIT) where he continued to research his Taylorist theories throughout the 1920s.

The inhumanity of Taylorism as communicated through Gastev and Proletkult was savagely parodied by Evgeny Zamyatin in *We* (1920). In this science-fiction novel he described a totally regulated world of the future where identical workers lived in glass-sided apartments and subordinated individual desires to the demands of the 'United State' and the regular timetable of industrial production. The broader implications of Zamyatin's novel as a critique of the whole Communist system were not missed by Glavlit (the vigilant state department of censorship) and although it was circulated widely in typescript *We* has still to be officially published within the Soviet Union.

Taylor's influence, however, was more strikingly felt in Meyerhold's avant-garde theatre than ever it was in the Soviet economy. His theories of rational and effective movement provided a framework for a new form of theatrical expression – biomechanics – which Meyerhold had combined with Pavlov's theories on psychological reflexes to create a form of acting which, stripped of intuition, seemed to be as efficient as an oiled machine. Declamatory and clown-like, this style furthered Meyerhold's move away from realism towards a more expressive theatre of symbols. The science of biomechanics was given a public première in 1922 in *The Magnanimous Cuckold* by Fernand Crommelynck and *Tarelkin's Death* by Alexander Sukhovo-Kobylin at the newly opened Actors' Theatre in Moscow. The machine-like sets were designed by the young Constructivist artists Liubov Popova and Varvara Stepanova. They were, according to Meyerhold, 'to lay the basis for a new form of theatrical presentation . . . making do with the simple objects which came to hand and transforming a spectacle performed by specialists into an improvised performance which could be put on by workers in their spare time.'

Taylorism was only a part of a general enthusiasm for American ideas and culture which pervaded Soviet culture during the 1920s. This admiration was based on the conviction that both countries were new worlds which had sloughed off the oppression of the old. The marvels of Henry Ford's production lines, the skyscrapers of New York, the girders of Brooklyn Bridge and the films of Sennett, Pickford, Fairbanks and Chaplin had all been created under the yoke of capitalism: how these could be surpassed under the glories of Communism!

The banana skin in history

The knockabout comedy of Hollywood two-reelers was of particular interest to the formalist school of writers in Opoyaz (the Association of Poetic Language) which, under the leadership of Viktor Shklovsky, Yuri Tynianov, Boris Eichenbaum and Ro-

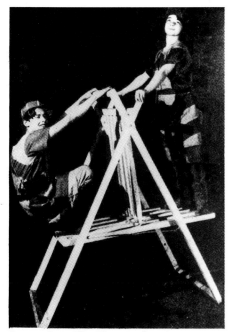

Scene from *The Magnanimous Cuckold*, 1922.

man Jakobson, had developed out of Futurism a critical theory concentrating on the subject of literary style devoid of associative meaning. These writers strove to create unusual effects to combat readers' automatic perceptions. Usual distinctions between form and content were swept away in the Formalist concept of the unitary artistic device. Such ideas, however, were not confined to this group and in 1922 in Petrograd a younger generation of actors, led by Gregory Kozintsev, Leonid Trauberg and Sergei Yutkevich, opened the Factory of the Eccentric Actor (FEKS). Influenced by Meyerhold, these actors developed an alogical style of movement and plot which owed more to the traditions of circus, music hall and the Hollywood chase than it did to traditional theatre. 'Yesterday the culture of Europe,' Kozintsev wrote in his 1922 manifesto, 'today the technology of America. . . . We prefer Charlie's backside to Eleonora Duse's hands: the play – an accumulation of tricks. The speed of 1000 horsepower. Chase, persecution, flight. Form – a divertissement. . . . THE AMERICANIZATION OF THE THEATRE in Russia means ECCentriSM.' In 1924 Kozintsev and Trauberg moved from theatre to film in *The Adventures of Oktyabrina,* the first in a long and successful collaboration. A similar debt to and satire of Hollywood was also evident in Lev Kuleshov's Soviet spoof thriller *The Strange Adventures of Mr West in the Land of the Bolsheviks,* also made in 1924, and in Boris Barnet's *Miss Mend* (1926), a cliff-hanger in three parts in which the Soviet heroine triumphs over Yankee Counter-Revolutionaries.

The film industry flourished throughout the whole of the USSR as well as in Moscow, under the stewardship of Sovkino – the state film industry – and Narkompros; active studios with individual regional styles grew up in Georgia and the Ukraine.

Trained in Meyerhold's Directors' Workshop as well as in the less grave environment of Baron Nikolai Foregger's satirical Studio Theatre, Sergei Eisenstein designed and directed a number of experimental plays for the Moscow Proletkult Central Workers' Theatre. Many of these used broken narrative, burlesque and circus tricks and were in conscious parody of the multiplicity of 'advanced' artistic styles which then proliferated. One of the most important of these productions was Sergei Tretiakov's adaptation of Alexander Ostrovsky's *Enough Stupidity in Every Wise Man* (1923) for which Eisenstein made his first film, *Glumov's Diary,* 120 metres long, to be integrated into the action. Because of a shortage of stock, there was no scope for wastage and the film had to be 'edited' in the camera. Prompted by this experience, Eisenstein published his first theoretical manifesto, *The Montage of Attractions,* in 1923 in the magazine *LEF* (an acronym for Left Front of the Arts). These theories, with their stress on the role of editing as a means of establishing a visual dialectic, put forward the idea that film 'must be a tendentious selection and juxtaposition, free from narrowly fictional tasks, moulding the audience in accordance with its goal'. In line with Lenin's directives of January 1920, film was to be a means of raising political consciousness in the masses. In April 1924 Eisenstein started work on *Strike,* his first full-length film, which was quickly followed by the international success of *The Battleship Potemkin* (1925).

Similar formal parallels can be seen in the art of

Rodchenko, cover for a cinema review, 1922.

Eisenstein with the crew of *The Battleship Potemkin* and a model of the ship, 1925.

Rodchenko, photomontage
for Mayakovsky's *About This*, 1923.

Vesnin (centre, with pipe) with
Popova and friends.
Photo by Rodchenko, 1923.

photomontage, to which a number of Constructivist artists turned as an alternative to painting. The disjointed images of Alexander Rodchenko's illustrations for Vladimir Mayakovsky's poem of unrequited love, *About This* (1923), can be viewed as part of an avant-garde tendency towards the re-orientation of the audience's expectations through alogical shifts of form and narrative.

New Economic Policy 1921-8

After the ravages of the Civil War which immediately followed the Revolution and the terrible Volga famine of 1921, Lenin had no alternative but to revive the failing economy by re-introducing private enterprise. He was acutely aware that the predictions of Marx had been made for advanced industrial countries; if they were to have any validity for Russia, Soviet society desperately needed time for mass education and for consolidation of its economy. The securing of reliable food supplies was an urgent priority so the co-operation of the countryside was bought by allowing the peasants to sell surplus products on the private market, and in the industrial sector the small family business was encouraged. The New Economic Policy (NEP), as this was called, lasted from 1921 to 1928 and coincided with a remarkable flowering of Soviet culture.

By early 1923, the leadership of the avant-garde in Moscow had been taken over by a group of writers, critics, poets and artists centred on the magazine *LEF* which, under the leadership of Osip Brik and Vladimir Mayakovsky, stressed the importance of researching new forms and means of expression in keeping with the technological age. Many of the LEF artists were affiliated to the Moscow Higher State Art and Technical Studios (Vkhutemas) which had taken over the premises of the pre-Revolutionary Stroganov School of Art and provided a training in specialist skills and basic design. Tatlin, Rodchenko, Stepanova, Popova, El Lissitzky, Alexander Vesnin and Moisei Ginsburg all taught there and independently developed an educational movement towards free creativity and functional design which rivalled that of the Bauhaus in Germany. It was by working directly in industry, film, photomontage, typography, architecture, design, photography and writing that artists were to effect the long-awaited combination of art with life under the banner of socialism. In 1924 Popova's and Stepanova's textile designs for the First Moscow Textile Factory were featured in *LEF* while other magazines, such as the similarly aligned *Red Virgin Soil*, published patterns for cheap-to-make fashions by the pre-Revolutionary couturier Nadezhda Lamanova, and by artists such as Alexandra Exter and Vera Mukhina. In the porcelain factories at Dulevo outside Moscow and at the former Imperial works in Petrograd, production was supervised by artists, many of whom were trained in the Moscow Vkhutemas or at the Leningrad Academy where a wide range of subjects which integrated the artist into industry as a designer were also taught.

Throughout the 1920s Vladimir Tatlin continued to work on practical projects as Director of the Petrograd Museum of Artistic Culture and later for the Moscow Vkhutemas, making designs for workers'

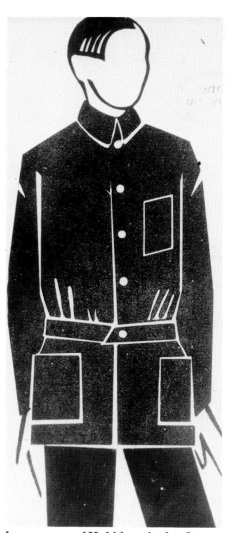

Lamanova and Mukhina, design for
'Tolstoy Tunic', 1926.

clothing, mass-produced ceramics and for high-efficiency stoves for heating apartments. His utopian ideals, however, remained and on returning to Moscow in 1929 he started to work on the development of a flying machine which could be cheaply made and widely distributed. He headed a small group of researchers at the Experimental Scientific Research Laboratory housed in the Novodevichy Monastery. 'I want to give back to man the feeling of flight,' he wrote. 'We have been robbed of this by the mechanical flight of the aeroplane. We cannot feel the movement of our body in the air.' The glider was to be 'an everyday object for the Soviet masses, an ordinary item of use . . . art is going out into technology.' The aim of this new art was an exploration of 'the organic relationship between materials and their handling'. The models and plans for *Letatlin*, as the flying machine was called – a play on the artist's own name and the Russian word *letat*, to fly – were widely exhibited and aroused much public interest. However, the research group was dissolved in 1932 together with all other artists' groups. This effectively spelled an end to the project and the critical flying test, as far as we know, never took place. Subsequently, working in isolation, Tatlin focused his attention increasingly on theatre design and easel painting.

From 1923 to 1929 Malevich, also as head of Ginkhuk (the Leningrad branch of the Institute of Artistic Culture), became increasingly concerned with a more practical resolution of Suprematist ideas. Working on ceramic designs for the Lomonosov Porcelain Factory and on a series of plaster and wood models called *architektons,* Malevich and his followers experimented with a new system of spatial relationships which, they felt, would reflect the transformed realities of the future. Less romantic and more scientific than the work of Unovis, these projects were developed into further models called *Planits* – projects for houses of the future – which in turn were then integrated into planning designs for satellite towns around Moscow. During the late 1920s Malevich also made designs for textiles and clothes. Yet in spite of their practical application, his ideas swam against the functionalist and Constructivist current. For him the artist, not the engineer, was the most important creator of the modern age who alone could discern 'the dynamic spiritual world of things'. Greater forces than need or function dominated society's desire for renewal and it was only through recognition of these forces that social harmony could be achieved.

In music Nikolai Rosavlets had taken up Scriabin's struggle to construct a new theory of harmony; he developed this into a twelve-note system which embraced elements of serialism. A confirmed Marxist, he believed that 'organized tonal matter' should fit into the new Communist world order. Anti-romanticism pervaded the music of the 1920s – from the Neo-classicism of Stravinsky, now in permanent voluntary exile, to the 'new objectivity' or 'linearity' of such composers as Alexander Mosolov and Vladimir Deshevov; industrial leitmotifs ran through the work of both. Mosolov's best-known work, *The Iron Foundry* (1927), was written in honour of the tenth anniversary of the October Revolution. Deshevov's phenomenally large output included the ballet *The Red Whirlwind* (1924) and the

Leonidov, model of Lenin Institute, 1927.

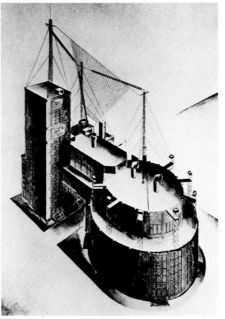

Vesnin brothers, design for Palace of Labour, 1922-3.

opera *Ice and Steel* (1930) as well as film, theatre and orchestral music. In 1925 the precocious Dmitri Shostakovich's First Symphony was such a success that he was commissioned to write a Second Symphony to commemorate the tenth anniversary of the Revolution; this incorporated the sound of a factory siren into the score. He also began to write music for films and the theatre, including Mayakovsky's new play *The Bedbug* (1928) and Kozintsev and Trauberg's film *New Babylon* (1929). In 1918 Sergei Prokofiev left Russia for a protracted concert tour in the West; he did not return to live there until 1932 but during his period of absence he was regarded in the West as a Bolshevik composer.

The new architecture of the 1920s became polarized between the 'rationalism' of Nikolai Ladovsky and the Asnova (New Association of Architects) group and the Constructivism of the Vesnin brothers and Moisei Ginsburg in OSA (the Union of Contemporary Architects). In 1923 Ladovsky, a professor in the Moscow Vkhutemas, with his colleagues Dokuchaev and Krinsky, advocated a synthesis of painting, sculpture and architecture. He adopted 'psycho-analytical' methods of researching architectural space and studying the physiological effects of shape and firmly believed that good new architecture rested on the fruitful collaboration between producer (architect) and consumer (the masses). Because of its experimental nature, much of Asnova's work remained on the drawing-board and did not progress beyond the level of academic research, although in the mid 1920s Ladovsky did make designs for prefabricated houses and later produced a planning scheme for the garden city development of greater Moscow.

The Constructivists centred on OSA were affiliated with the LEF group and were primarily concerned with problems of housing and the communal conception of society; a number of important public buildings were completed by them. They favoured a functional rather than an intuitive approach and criticized the Asnova architects for their old-fashioned ideas and lack of practical work. While the Vesnin brothers designed the first generally acknowledged Constructivist buildings – the competition design for the Palace of Labour (1922-3) – Moisei Ginsburg was the chief propagandist. In articles in the magazine *Contemporary Architecture* (1923) and in his book *Style and Epoch* (1924), he stressed the technological basis of the new forms and his desire to integrate new scientific and technical discoveries into the discipline of modern architecture; this he called 'the mechanization of life'. Such views were close to those of Le Corbusier in France and, not surprisingly, the French architect was made an affiliate of OSA and subsequently in 1928 was invited by the state to design the Centrosoyuz building in Moscow.

Alternatives

Not all artists, however, were seduced by the progressive or iconoclastic tendencies of Constructivism and throughout the 1920s a number of groups of realist artists were formed which took a more literal view of the task of depicting the new society. One of these was the New Society of Painters (NOZh), which **21** included former pupils of Exter, Malevich and Tatlin, who confessed in the catalogue for their first exhibition in 1922: 'We, former leftists in art, were the first to feel the utter rootlessness of further analytical and scholastic aberrations . . . for Constructivism, in proclaiming the death of art, conceived man as an automaton.'

The more conservatively based Association of Artists of Revolutionary Russia (AKhRR) absorbed many of the surviving Wanderers as well as defected 'Cézannists' – former members of the Jack of Diamonds; they declared their opposition to the leftist Constructivists. Their aim, as stated at their first exhibition in 1922, was to 'depict the present day: the life of the Red Army, the workers, the peasants, the revolutionaries and the heroes of labour'. By the mid 1920s it had become the largest artists' organization within the Soviet Union, with regional and youth groups throughout the country and its own publishing house and, from 1929, its own magazine, *Art for the Masses*. Many of its members were the mainstay of the Union of Artists after the reorganization of literary-artistic organizations in 1932 and subsequently could be described as Socialist Realists.

In 1925 another group of figurative painters founded OST (The Society of Easel Painters) which provided a focus for artists, like Alexander Deineka, Yuri Pimenov, David Shterenberg and Alexander Tyshler, who wished to find new forms of realism.

Foreign films, particularly those from Hollywood, were imported in considerable numbers until 1928; total box office receipts for these outstripped those for home-produced films. Given the choice, the majority of the Soviet public preferred Charlie Chaplin, Douglas Fairbanks or Buster Keaton to Sergei Eisenstein or Vsevolod Pudovkin. Many foreign writers also continued to appear in translation: between 1923 and 1930 over a hundred Western science-fiction titles appeared, excluding the already popular works of Jules Verne and H.G. Wells.

During the 1920s there was a constant flux of re-orientating groups and exhibiting societies and a remarkable diversity throughout Soviet culture. At the extremes of the avant-garde, 'nothingists' on one side faced 'everythingists' on the other. Other conflicts absorbed the Communist Party: both the right wing, exemplified in the beliefs of Nikolai Bukharin, and the left wing, as represented by Leon Trotsky, strongly supported cultural pluralism, although for different reasons. Realist proletarian movements such as RAPP (the Russian Association of Proletarian Writers), founded in 1922, AKhRR and the October Group, founded in 1923, did not take such a flexible view and all virulently attacked whatever they identified as bourgeois, élitist, formalist and avant-garde. As head of Narkompros, the Commissariat of Enlightenment, Lunacharsky had carefully and diplomatically tried to maintain a creative tension between conservative and radical factions, not giving preference to any one interest. In the harder political climate of the late 1920s, however, such professional neutrality was no longer tenable. In 1929 Lunacharsky resigned from his post and Stalin began to engineer the future development of Soviet culture to satisfy his own ends.

Stalin was able to do this because Lenin's ideas on cultural policy had never been properly codified and at different times he had even urged opposing

'At the wheel', 1931. Photo by Shaikhet.

Stalin at the 1938 Party Congress.

opinions. After Lenin's death in 1924 these ambiguities had provided ammunition for all interests who wished to seek precedents for their own opinions in his writings. Like Lenin, Bukharin strongly supported a gradual evolution of society. He felt that the mixed economy and culture of the New Economic Policy should be indefinitely extended to give time for the development of heavy industry and provide a breathing space for the peasantry – still by far the largest mass of the population – to achieve political and cultural maturity. This was in line with the predictions of Marx for whom revolution was unthinkable without a large urban proletariat.

Trotsky, on the other hand, was less prepared to wait and applauded the constructive influence of avant-garde art on the rapid development of Soviet culture and attitudes. In *Literature and Revolution* (1923) he denied the need for, or possibility of, any exclusively 'proletarian culture' and denounced those who supported these ideas as retrograde. Culture, for Trotsky, had a latitude which need not be confined by politics; art, he felt, should be allowed to flourish without undue interference from governments; the intelligentsia and 'fellow-travellers' were to be encouraged as those 'who, staggering and stumbling, go up to a certain point along that same road which we shall travel much further'.

As Party Secretary Stalin manipulated the split, siding at first with Bukharin to isolate the leftists until by 1925 the Left had lost all say in formulating policy; in 1927 Trotsky and his supporters were expelled from the Party and in 1929 Trotsky was deported. From that time Trotskyism began to be equated with 'leftist avant-gardism and cosmopolitanism' and the cultural diversity which had so characterized the 1920s came increasingly under threat. Bukharin, similarly, was quickly discredited as Stalin moved closer to complete personal control of the Party; his followers were criticized as rightists, and the aesthetic bedfellows of the New Economic Policy who were identified with him were denounced as 'fellow-travellers' and formalists.

Stalin could now consolidate his power and move away from the views of the Right to put forward a radical programme for the collectivization of agriculture and the development of heavy industry which, in its speed of execution and lack of regard for human suffering, exceeded the most radical policies of the Left Opposition. In August 1928 the first Five Year Plan was enthusiastically adopted by the Fifteenth Party Conference. Given this mandate, collectivization and industrialization proceeded at breakneck speed. By the end of 1931, 20,000,000 individual farms had been amalgamated into 250,000 collectives through the use of force as peasants burnt crops and slaughtered livestock rather than hand them over: the resulting famine claimed even more lives. Industrialization was also achieved at the cost of brutal compulsion, with convicts used as forced labour on such projects as the economically worthless White Sea/Baltic Canal. However, despite poor resources and a ragged labour force great steps forward were made in the building of heavy industries and hydro-electric power plants. Every sinew was strained to fulfil the slogan '5 in 4' as the objectives of the first plan were achieved in 1932, within four years.

The Cultural Revolution 1928-32

As Stalin manoeuvred to gain complete control of the Party he began to rewrite history to place himself as the one and only heir to the legacy of Marx, Engels and Lenin. Accordingly, he initiated what has been called the Cultural Revolution which, by strengthening the hand of the proletarian art movements in painting, music, architecture and film, effectively removed the last vestiges of independence in the arts and opened the way for the monolithic doctrine of Socialist Realism.

The first All Union Party Conference on Film Questions, held in March 1928, cast its lot in favour of popularism when it called for fictional films to be 'made in a way that can be appreciated by millions'. Yet in calling for this, they were not responding to popular demand but rather advocating that films should be an instrument of ideology which would further the regeneration of Soviet society. In the final editing of *The General Line* (1929), Sergei Eisenstein's film on the impact of the first Five Year Plan on the countryside, Stalin himself directly intervened to change its ending: an epilogue was added to divert attention from the personal relationship of the two leading characters to the generalized moral of the natural bond between peasant and worker. In the authorities' eyes this epilogue was only partly successful and the film's relationship to Party policy was minimized by the choice of a less specific title, *The Old and the New,* under which it was released later in the year.

The confusion continued. In the summer of 1928, the All Union Conference on Propaganda and Agitation had bolstered the growing hysteria against 'formalism, constructivism and nihilism' without giving adequate guidelines as to what was acceptable policy. The result was chaos. Non-proletarian writers such as Mayakovsky, Yuri Olesha, Mikhail Bulgakov, Boris Pilnyak, Isaac Babel and Evgeny Zamyatin were all criticized by RAPP for their individualist, negative or leftist attitudes. In their self-consciously serious and bureaucratic view, art should be devoted to the depiction of socialist struggle to which the genre of satire could do nothing but harm. Mayakovsky's two satirical plays, *The Bedbug* (1928) and *The Bathhouse* (1930), with their outspoken criticism of opportunists, bureaucrats and time-servers, entered Meyerhold's repertoire to be heavily criticized by RAPP critics. In February 1930 Mayakovsky responded by holding an exhibition, called *Twenty Years of Work,* at the Union of Writers in Moscow. 'This exhibition is not a jubilee but an account rendered of my work,' he wrote sternly in the introduction. 'The point is to show that the writer-revolutionary is not alienated . . . [but] participates in everyday ordinary life and in the construction of Socialism.' Except for his LEF colleagues, the exhibition was virtually boycotted by the entire literary establishment in Moscow as well as in Leningrad where it was subsequently shown. The tide was running against him. The April issue of the new magazine *The Press and Revolution* was to include a photograph and 'Greetings to Mayakovsky – great Revolutionary poet' but this was cut out of the already

Bulgakov with friend, 1928.

Interior of Melnikov's Leyland bus garage, Moscow, 1926. Photo by Rodchenko.

printed edition on the order of the head of Gosizdat, the state publishing house. Depressed by this and by complications in his personal life, Mayakovsky shot himself on 14 April, the first casualty in the bitter struggle for artistic autonomy. Tatlin designed his catafalque. Thousands attended his funeral but for six years his work was officially disregarded until it was reinstated in *Pravda,* the Party newspaper, on the express wish of Stalin.

In the same year the Vkhutemas, or Vkhutein as it had been renamed, was closed down. Mayakovsky's colleagues on the magazine *Novy LEF* were also denounced for formalism and leftist tendencies. Alexander Rodchenko's steeply angled photographs were criticized in the magazine *Soviet Photography* for their subservience to foreign influences as well as for their obsession with the 'how' of photography rather than the 'what'. The issue of subject-matter versus style was critical to an understanding of this debate, the argument being whether new views and ways of seeing were necessary to express the changed reality of Soviet society. For Rodchenko and Sergei Tretiakov, co-editor of *Novy LEF,* the artist was a reporter, bringing alive the struggles of working people, reporting the facts of their lives; but, as proletarian groups throughout the arts became more vociferous, attitudes hardened and formal innovations of all kinds, which even Rodchenko later dismissed as 'the easel-painting mentality', were hysterically denounced. In 1929 and 1930 Rodchenko underwent a public transformation when he worked as a photojournalist documenting the building of the White Sea Canal in the far north: 'I was taken aback,' he wrote, 'I was seized with enthusiasm . . . I began to take pictures without any thought of formalism.' In those dark, inhumane and bitterly cold conditions he underwent a transformation rather like that of the convicts who were building the canal:

they [the critics] were saying 'renounce Formalism and go and work'. On the canal that was not an issue. A bandit was not set to work at a book-keeper's desk or a thief to issue papers or a prostitute to do the laundry. The bandit became a demolition worker, a shock worker or a member of an emergency brigade. The thief and embezzler they made club leader, a clerk or a purchasing agent. And they worked miracles.

Rodchenko's photographs were published in a special White Sea Canal edition of the new magazine *USSR in Construction* which documented progress in the Five Year Plans.

Many painters, writers, musicians and film-makers underwent the same kind of transformation and, following the advice of Comrade Stalin, decided that they 'should not invent images and events . . . [but] take them from life – learn from life. Let life teach you.' Artists joined brigades of workers on building sites, in factories, on collective farms, and their paintings recorded the construction of the new order. Valentin Katayev's new novel *Forward Time* (1932) chronicled one day of production in a large coke chemical plant. But at this time realism was not yet inextricably bound up with the doctrine of 'revolutionary romanticism' and there was still room for the transcendent and the expressive. In Leningrad the Masters of Analytical Art group founded by Pavel **23**

Nikritin, *Screaming Woman*, 1928.

Filonov continued until 1932 but his 1930 Russian Museum Exhibition was never opened to the public although it had been hung. Filonov's mystical, at times ambivalent, vision of the city and of the development of man did not in the words of one bureaucrat 'express clearly a correct, healthy psycho-ideological emphasis as well as a social orientation'. In Moscow both Alexander Drevin and Solomon Nikritin independently developed poetic and expressive styles which suggested doubt and dislocation in place of the officially approved empty and vainglorious heroism.

Malevich and his followers were also influenced by the changed temper of these times. Nikolai Suetin, who was working as an artist at the Leningrad Lomonosov Porcelain Factory, designed a number of Suprematist industrial motifs for ceramics: the best examples are the coffee sets 'Industry' (1929) and 'Agrogorod' ('Tractor Station') (1930) in which the simplified forms of Suprematism are now given a figurative reference. A similar shift took place in Malevich's own work and late in 1931 he was to write to a friend in Kiev: 'I am thinking of undertaking some painting, of doing some symbolic pictures. I am trying to produce an image.' In doing this he looked back to his early Neo-Primitivist and Cubo-Futurist work and began to work on a series of strongly frontal hieratic portraits which combine a simplified modern approach with references to the art of the northern Renaissance. The restless pursuit of a universal system, which had characterized the whole of the Russian avant-garde, here became subsumed within an historical eclecticism. In this way Malevich's circular path back towards his origins unconsciously prefigured the recent death of the 'progressive' Western avant-garde and the consequential birth of Post-Modernism.

Yet the subject matter of Malevich's late paintings can also be regarded as a response to the pressure to paint ideologically correct themes – the peasants in these pictures are representations of the new Soviet man and woman. Similarly his large semi-abstract painting *The Red Cavalry* which was not exhibited until 1932 represents a scene from the Civil War – the historical precedent which Stalin had cited for the titanic struggle of the Five Year Plans. Civil War themes and metaphors were rife in officially patronized polemic, literature and art. In painting they reached a ghastly apotheosis in Mitrofan Grekhov's heroic genre scenes of the First Cavalry Regiment, a travesty of realism when compared with the surgical irony of Isaac Babel's short stories on the same theme.

Many writers also felt under threat and began to modify their positions: in 1932 Yuri Olesha, author of the satirical novel *Envy* (1927), launched an essay in a confessional genre which was to become increasingly widespread – 'The Necessity of [Self] Reconstruction is Obvious to Me'. With the benefit of hindsight, Viktor Shklovsky too was able to write about this time: 'We former members of LEF took what was useful from life, thinking that this was aesthetic, we Constructivists created a construction that proved to be non-constructive.' The theme of economic and social transformation permeates the literature of the Cultural Revolution, from Boris Pilnyak's much-criticized novel of the first Five Year Plan *The Volga Falls into the Caspian Sea* (1930) to Bruno

Gerasimov, *Oath of the Siberian Partisans*, 1933.

Grekhov, *Machine-gun Cart*, 1925.

Jasiensky's self-explanatory *A Man Changes his Skin* (1934).

Not all writers, however, were able to weather these changes with ease. The Acme poets, Anna Akhmatova and Osip Mandelstam, with their emphasis on personal feelings at the expense of collective values, were open to criticism from the establishment. This, along with her first marriage to fellow poet Nikolai Gumilov, who had been shot in 1921 as a White collaborator, meant that Akhmatova's work was not published and that she and her family were constantly under suspicion. Mandelstam fared worse: his lyric poetry was so evidently out of step with the new Soviet era that during the second half of the 1920s he was able to write only prose. In 1930 he started to write poetry again in reaction to a systematic campaign of vilification in the Press; one of the poems was an epigram denouncing Stalin as a murderer and megalomaniac and although, of course, he did not offer it for publication, its existence was discovered and in 1934 he was thrown into prison. He was spared his life only through the direct intercession of Bukharin, Akhmatova and Boris Pasternak. Instead he was condemned to exile in Voronezh until 1937. Pasternak's poetry also was suspect and was roundly dismissed both by the Writers' Union and the Press for its 'bourgeois individualism'; from 1936 to 1943 he was allowed to publish nothing except translations.

The increased regimentation in the arts did not dissuade Sergei Prokofiev from returning to live in the Soviet Union in 1932 after fourteen years' absence. The popularist incidental music to the film *Lieutenant Kizhe* (1933) was one of his first new works. A new popular style of music began to be developed by Isaac Dunaevsky in 'Hollywood-style' musical comedy films such as *The Jolly Fellows* (1934) and the phenomenally popular *Volga-Volga* (1938) both directed by Grigory Alexandrov, Eisenstein's former assistant.

The agent of the Cultural Revolution in architecture was VOPRA (The All Union Association of Proletarian Architects), founded in 1929 under the leadership of the Armenian architect, Karo Alabian. Its All Union constitution meant that it included a large delegation of architects from the Republics, many of whom hated the metropolitan bias of the Constructivists, whom they felt had been unfairly favoured on their own territory. Formalist architects such as Konstantin Melnikov and Iakov Chernikov were also criticized because their emphasis on sculptural form in architecture left little scope for the ethnic traditions which architects from the Republics preferred.

The architecture of the avant-garde, however, like the art, literature and films, did not remain static during the Cultural Revolution and responded to the changed political climate with a move away from functionalism towards *gravitas* and monumentality. This is already clear in Melnikov's project for an unbuilt Monument to Christopher Columbus (1929), as it is in Iakov Chernikov's theoretical treatises and imaginative *Architectural Romances,* a series of drawings which he started in 1930. Architecture, it was agreed, had to serve the new society yet there was no consensus about what path should be taken. There were many vague, high-flown concepts: in 1929 the straightforward development of a site plan for Moscow's proposed Central Park of Culture and

Still from *Volga Volga*, directed by Alexandrov, 1938.

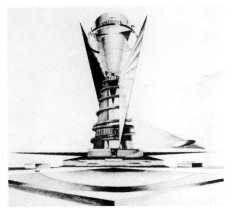

Melnikov, project for Monument to Christopher Columbus, 1929.

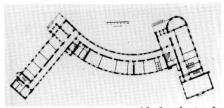

Nikolsky, plan for school in Leningrad, 1926-7.

Rest was transformed into an exercise for the creation of a space fit for the 'new Soviet man'. Attempts were made to find a new symbolism in architecture, the form reflecting not the function but the idea of the building as in Alexander Nikolsky's plan for a school in Leningrad built round the form of the hammer and sickle or, more magnificently, Melnikov's project for the Headquarters of the People's Commissariat for Heavy Industry (Narkomtiazprom) in 1934 which, in both plan and elevation, reflected twice over the dynamic thrust of the Roman numeral V – the monumental expression of each of the Five Year Plans. Such artifice as this, however, could be easily denounced as formalist – a charge which Karo Alabian's star-shaped Red Army Theatre of 1935-40, the five points of which were completely encompassed by a Neoclassical colonnade, managed to escape. But Melnikov had been too successful abroad and this, with his uncompromising manner, had singled him out as a 'recalcitrant anti-proletarian' and eventually led to his expulsion from the Union of Architects.

Increasingly during the first Five Year Plan the status of the architect had been eroded, as the initiative for the shaping of the new society was taken up by the engineer – the builders and designers of the new hydro-electric plants and heavy industries. Formal innovation had become politically suspect and the art of revivalism was all that remained. As a result, much time was spent by architects' groups in identifying scapegoats and defining what they were not, rather than in searching for a positive role in which to reassert their position.

Into the abyss

In 1932 the factionalism and confusions of the Cultural Revolution were brought to an end by the Party Central Committee decision on the reformation of literary-artistic organizations; this dissolved the many existing artists' groups and amalgamated them into Unions for each discipline. Since Lunacharsky's resignation from the Commissariat of Enlightenment in 1929, the formulation of artistic policy had become the province of Stalin himself and of his son-in-law Andrei Zhdanov, who had been promoted to Party Secretary. A blatant and unashamed Philistine – 'Pushkin is of lesser importance than a good pair of boots' – Stalin set out to subordinate all cultural life to the objectives of the Party. From the beginning of the first Five Year Plan to its completion – one year early – in 1932, Party membership virtually trebled and it was upon this base of newly recruited workers that Stalin was able to extend his personal power. The Seventeenth Party Congress in January 1934 was hailed as 'the Congress of Victors', the defeat of the enemies of the Soviet Union was celebrated and the first phase of industrialization was complete. Yet behind this presentation of monolithic concord an opposition to the consolidation of Stalin's personal power was gathering momentum. This was centred on Sergei Kirov, the Party Secretary in Leningrad, and on the veteran and discredited Revolutionary Bukharin. By the end of the year Kirov had been assassinated and the opposition had evaporated. Over 70 per cent of the Central Committee which **25** was elected at this Congress was, during the next five years, to face the firing squad in the horrific series of purges which ensued.

Later in 1934 at the first All Union Congress of Soviet Writers, the Party's domination of all cultural life was confirmed when the tendency of Socialist Realism was codified by Zhdanov and Maxim Gorky into a method: 'the Party is organizing the masses for the struggle to destroy capitalist elements once and for all, and to eradicate the last vestiges of capitalism in our economy and in people's minds.' This could only be achieved 'under the great banner of Marx-Engels-Lenin-Stalin'. Socialist Realism was to be an organ of class struggle and a non-tendentious literature could not be allowed to exist. The writer was, in Stalin's words, to be 'an engineer of human souls' who should depict life 'in its revolutionary development'. Its genre would be 'revolutionary romanticism' in which 'Soviet literature must be able to show our heroes and catch a glimpse of our tomorrow. This will not be a utopia, because our tomorrow is being prepared today by our systematic and conscious work.' This programme was to be limited not only to literature but applied systematically throughout the arts.

Realist painters and sculptors, former members of AKhRR, such as Isaac Brodsky, Director of the new All Russian Academy of Arts, and Alexander Gerasimov, his successor, continued to work more or less untroubled by the shotgun marriage of aesthetics with Party ideology, but for others conformity was less easy to achieve. Isaac Babel dryly observed that henceforth he would have to observe 'the genre of silence' – a genre that was soon to gain more widespread acceptance.

At this time, Sergei Eisenstein was working with Isaac Babel on a script for *Bezhin Meadow*, from a Turgenev short story, and was under severe criticism for his concentration on the moral rather than the realist aspects of the adaptation; in 1937 all work on the film was halted at the express wish of Boris Shumyatsky, the head of the Soviet film industry. Zhdanov also continued to intervene directly in artistic policy. In January 1936 in an article in *Pravda* entitled 'Noise instead of Music', he denounced Dmitri Shostakovich's opera *Lady Macbeth of Mtsensk* (1932) as 'un-Soviet, unwholesome, cheap, eccentric, tuneless and leftist'. Two months later, in the same paper, in an article headed 'On Slovenly Artists', he ominously proclaimed that formalism would not 'get the patronage of the Soviet people' and heralded a purge of deviant painters, musicians and cultural figures. Shostakovich responded quickly, and late in 1937 he reappeared with his Fifth Symphony subtitled 'A Soviet Artist's Reply to Just Criticism'.

Others were not so fortunate in being accepted. Alexander Mosolov was expelled from the Union of Composers in 1936 and Konstantin Melnikov was dismissed from the Union of Architects. Yet the witch-hunt against formalism and leftism continued to even greater lengths. Previous supporters of Party doctrine were given no immunity from prosecution and fell alongside the avant-garde: Leopold Averbakh, the leader of RAPP until its dissolution in 1932, was shot for leftism in 1938; Boris Shumyatsky, saboteur of *Bezhin Meadow*, whose ambition was to build a film factory – a 'Soviet Hollywood' on the Black Sea, was sacked for incompetence and subsequently shot; in 1939 Vsevolod Meyerhold was arrested and shot, and his wife, the actress Zinaida Raikh, was discovered brutally murdered in their Moscow flat; in 1938 Osip Mandelstam died in a transit camp after having been arrested and exiled a second time; Boris Pilnyak went missing in 1939; the writer, critic and playwright Sergei Tretiakov was arrested and shot for leftist tendencies and his wife Olga was consigned to the Gulag; Isaac Babel disappeared in a Gulag some time in 1941 as did the Constructivist Gustav Klutsis in 1944. Many others perished. Those that survived did so by luck, humiliating public recantation of previous beliefs, or by uncritical adherence to the Party line. The idealism and energy of the Revolutionary avant-garde were tragically stillborn; the visionary new world which they themselves had helped to build now stood in ruins; their dreams of the future had mutated from a utopia into a nightmare.

Shostakovich, c. 1937.

A SEARCH FOR IDENTITY

Nationalism and realism at the turn of the century

Bridging the void between the exotic past and the modern world, Russia was suffering a crisis of identity. The Imperial Russian Pavilion and extensive related displays at the Eleventh Paris World Exhibition in 1900 gave full voice to the search for Slav roots which typified much Russian art and design during the closing years of the nineteenth century. This quest was part of a broader, Pan-Slavist political movement: the work traversed the fine and decorative arts and architecture to touch on stage design and music. It was based upon the revival of national building types, traditional decorative motifs and, in painting, upon subjects which referred to the once-glorious history and soul of the Slavs. At its most extravagant it found expression in the richly decorated traditional Boyar costumes worn by the tsarist court.

Victor Vasnetsov, painter, decorative artist and architect, was one of the leading figures in this revival. His best-known paintings are based on themes from the Lays – ancient Russian poems in which the warrior is seen as the defender of civilization against the encroachment of Mongol hordes. One of his leading patrons was Savva Mamontov, speculator and railway magnate; Vasnetsov designed the church and its iconostasis for Mamontov's estate at Abramtsevo near Zagorsk, where he had a studio from the mid 1870s.

Mikhail Vrubel, eight years younger than Vasnetsov, was also closely associated with Abramtsevo and worked there on ceramics and stage designs. In such paintings as *The Demon Seated* (1890), *The Demon Outcast* (1902) and *Pan* (1899) he developed a mystical and intuitive view of the Slavic soul. Inspired by Mikhail Lermontov's poem, 'The Demon', this fixation with the symbol of man fallen from grace remained with him until his death from syphilis in 1910.

If the nationalist movement in art can be seen as a form of escapism, harking to the past, then the alternative, for some, lay in a direct critique of modern society. The social novel was well established in Russian literature and throughout the arts there had developed a utilitarian tendency which held that the function of art was not the elevation of beauty but the critical exposure of social inequality. A group of painters called the Wanderers – which included Ilya Repin, Vladimir Makovsky and Abram Arkhipov – consciously adopted this programme and were encouraged by the enthusiastic patronage of Pavel Tretiakov, one of the leading collectors of late nineteenth-century Russian realist painting.

A similar mood was prevalent in drama. The move towards a more accurate realism in Konstantin Stanislavsky's Moscow Arts Theatre was strengthened by a psychologically aware, non-declamatory style of acting. They staged new plays by both Chekhov and Gorky, which clinically exposed the moral paralysis of the liberal intelligentsia.

Lev Tolstoy, novelist, essayist and vegetarian, at his country estate of Yasnaya Polyana in winter 1909. Tolstoy believed in the instinctive nobility of 'simple' living and he self-consciously lived a 'peasant' life on his estate. Art should also be simple and widely accessible, he felt, and should evoke moral feelings in its audience. One year after this photograph was taken, dogged by perpetual domestic disputes, he fled his home and died shortly afterwards at the railside halt of Astapovo.

**Victor Vasnetsov,
Knight at the Crossroads, 1882.**

**Ivan Bilibin, 'Knight at the Crossroads',
an illustration for *Tsarevich Ivan,
the Firebird and the Gray Wolf*, 1899.**

**Nikolai Roerich, 'The Camp of the
Polovtsy', design for Borodin's opera
Prince Igor, 1909.**

Victor Vasnetsov's *Knight at the Crossroads* (1882) became one of the most famous paintings of the Slavic revival. This central theme of a turning point in Russian history, which had considerable contemporary reverberations, is echoed in Ivan Bilibin's illustrations for the fairy tale *Tsarevich Ivan, the Firebird and the Gray Wolf* (1899). Bilibin joined the World of Art group and became particularly well known for his illustrations of children's books.

Traditional Slavic themes also became popular in opera and ballet, as in Nikolai Roerich's design 'The Camp of the Polovtsy' for Borodin's opera *Prince Igor* (1909). Mikhail Vrubel's atmospheric painting of the god *Pan* (1899) also looks back to a mythic age of primitive forces. A proto-Modernist, Vrubel sought to harmonize figures within their landscape by using strong ambient moods of colour. Less of a realist than Vasnetsov, he revealed in the mosaic-like structures, freer handling and decorative scale of his paintings an aspiration towards the analogy of music: in their reliance on mood above content they prefigured the work of the Symbolists.

Mikhail Vrubel, *Pan*, 1899. ▶

Tsar Nicholas II, the Empress Alexandra and members of the Court in the Hermitage Theatre, St Petersburg, February 1903.

Escapism and nostalgia were clearly represented in the opulence of the Imperial Court which, during the first decade of the century, was becoming increasingly isolated. In 1913 the 300th anniversary of the Romanov dynasty was celebrated, yet such was the mood of the country that this was not an occas-
ion for widespread rejoicing. Within the confines of the Palace, wearing the richly decorated Boyar costumes of the sixteenth and seventeenth centuries, the Tsar and his Court remained aloof from the massive social changes which had started to take place in Russia.

Portrait photo of the Emperor and Empress, 1903.

APANAGES IMPÉRIAUX

In 1900 Konstantin Korovin, painter, stage designer and architect, was, with fellow artist-designer Alexander Golovin, asked to act as artistic adviser to the Russian section of the Paris World Exhibition. He specially designed a number of small wooden pavilions which housed displays of folk arts, crafts and icons. The grand scale of the main pavilion in the Trocadero was, however, less successful in its eclectic and inelegant combination of high 'Kremlin' wall and towers with traditional and vernacular styles. In his search for a cultural identity, Korovin had created a spurious, backward-looking image of Russia. The new railways, the chemical and metallurgical industries, the mineral, forestry and fur trades upon which the country's wealth was based were all represented, yet within an exotic context that made few concessions to the modern world. There was one incongruous exception: a pavilion of galoshes which housed a rubber mountain of 35,000 pairs of boots, the product of one day's output at the Russian-American Rubber Company.

Feodor Shekhtel also adopted the forms of national architecture for the four wooden pavilions he designed for the Glasgow International Exhibition of 1901. Here ethnic and religious models from the north of Russia were combined with Art Nouveau to create what the critic for *The Art Journal* unfairly described as 'an architectural nightmare'.

The 'Paris Kremlin', the Siberian pavilion at the Eleventh World Exhibition, Paris 1900.

Russian section in the Palace of Chemical Industries at the Eleventh World Exhibition.
◀ **Siberian pavilion, Paris 1900.**

Shekhtel's pavilion devoted to the mining industries in the Russian section of the Glasgow International Exhibition, 1901.

Maxim Dmitriev was one of the pioneers of photographic journalism in Russia whose earlier work had been strongly influenced by the genre subjects of the Wanderers. He worked mostly in the area of Nizhny-Novgorod in northern Russia, where he had his studio, and also in the Volga valley, where he made a number of working trips.

In 1891 there was a disastrous famine in the Volga, followed in the next year by epidemics of cholera and typhus. Dmitriev documented this, showing the plight of the people, the miserable conditions in which they lived, their sense of helplessness: even the thatched roofs had been stripped of straw in order to feed the dwindling livestock (*inset*). In Nizhny-Novgorod Dmitriev became friendly with the writer Maxim Gorky, who was then working as a journalist. Their association continued and in 1902, when Gorky was preparing his play *The Lower Depths* for production in Stanislavsky's new Moscow Arts Theatre, he asked Dmitriev for photographs of social types which he could show to the actors and costume designer to give them an idea of how he conceived their parts and appearances.

Three photos by Maxim Dmitriev. Workers in a boiler factory, c. 1890. *Inset:* Living conditions during the Volga famine of 1891-2.

Vladimir Makovsky,
The Evening Meeting, **1897.**

Art, it was felt, had to have a moral and social purpose. The Wanderers wanted to show reality in all its harshness to expose the inequalities in Russian society. *The Evening Meeting,* Makovsky's study of late nineteenth-century intellectuals and activists, captures their febrile energy and disillusionment as reform gave way to an increasingly hard autocracy.

◀ **Abram Arkhipov,** *Laundresses,* **1901.**

The Wanderers, Moscow 1886. Makovsky is seated fourth from the left. Ilya Repin, also seated, is third from the right.

Pavel Tretiakov, patron of the Wanderers, talking to Nikolai Gritsenko (left), an artist, in St Petersburg, c. 1893.

Nikolai Roerich painting the apse of the Talashkino estate church, 1890s.

Valentin Serov, *Madame Orlova*, 1911.

Leon Bakst, *Portrait of Sergei Diaghilev with his Nurse*, 1906.

Modern art was patronized and encouraged by a small group of important collectors. Savva Mamontov and the Princess Tenisheva both formed colonies of like-minded artists at their country estates at Abramtsevo and Talashkino; both encouraged the revival of national styles and folk art.

Sergei Diaghilev reacted against the earnest realism of the Wanderers: 'It's time for these anti-artistic canvases to stop – with their militiamen, police officers, students in red shirts and girls with red hair.' His mercurial career as exhibition organizer, founder of the World of Art group in St Petersburg in 1898 and publisher of its magazine, covered both national and international styles. He played a decisive role in the introduction of modern Western art into Russia.

Mikhail Vrubel, *Portrait of Savva* ▶ *Mamontov, 1897.*

Gorky and other members of the Wednesday Circle, Moscow 1902. *Sitting:* Leonid Andreev, Feodor Shalyapin (opera singer and protégé of Mamontov), Ivan Bunin, Nikolai Teleshov (founder of the Circle), E. Chirikov. *Standing:* Skitalets (S. Petrov), Maxim Gorky.

Anna Golubkina, *The Wave*, new Moscow Arts Theatre.

Scene from Stanislavsky's production of Gogol's *The Government Inspector*, Moscow Arts Theatre 1908.

Scene from Stanislavsky's production of Gorky's *The Lower Depths*, Moscow Arts Theatre 1902.

Realism in literature began to assume a cutting edge. The writings of Anton Chekhov, Maxim Gorky and the members of the Wednesday Circle in Moscow ironically exposed the rottenness within society and contrasted the deprivations and common sense of working people with the confusion and guilt of the intelligentsia. In 1898 Konstantin Stanislavsky, a cousin of Savva Mamontov, founded the Moscow Arts Theatre which premièred the plays of Chekhov and Gorky. Here Stanislavsky pioneered a new style of acting which emphasized naturalistic detail as well as the psychological motivation of the characters.

In 1909 the architect Feodor Shekhtel was invited to convert the old Lianozovsky Theatre as a new centre for the Moscow Arts Theatre. Stanislavsky described Shekhtel's plan as of 'extraordinary simplicity'; one of the few decorative elements was Anna Golubkina's relief *The Wave,* over the main entrance.

◀ Maxim Gorky, Nizhny-Novgorod *c.*1903. Photo by Dmitriev.

Anton Chekhov and Lev Tolstoy, 1901. Photo by Dmitriev.

THE BANKRUPT SOCIETY

Crumbling Empire and the birth of a new consciousness

Throughout Europe the first decade of the twentieth century saw a challenge to the rigid hierarchical values of the past. Radical political movements flourished; women fought for greater sexual, economic and legal freedom; the young rebelled against the authority of their parents; pioneering discoveries in philosophy, psychology and physics, by figures such as Bergson, Jung, Pavlov and Einstein, swept away pre-existing notions of the causes of human behaviour and our place in the universe.

During the nineteenth century inflexible autocracy and the lack of an influential middle class had insulated tsarist Russia from the cultural ferment which was experienced in the rest of Europe; but by 1900 the tide could no longer be stemmed and a sense of instability swept across the country. Social unrest and strikes; a humiliating defeat by the Japanese in 1905; brutal pogroms by the government-supported Black Hundreds; and the savage repression of all opposition, were not mitigated by the paper reforms wrested from the Tsar in the aftermath of the 1905 Revolution. There was a pervasive hunger for change which fed the desire for experiment in art. The old order was rotten and everything connected with it seemed to be hopelessly tainted – new forms had to be found.

Artists began to explore different ways of depicting experience. Many wished to move away from the portrayal of the literary or the narrative to express a transcendent reality, and they began to develop alternative forms of expression and to search for a unity between the arts. Art became the representation not of life as it was perceived but as it was felt. At a time when the fabric of society was falling apart, many artists devoted their lives to the pursuit of spiritual values. The rich, liberal Moscow merchants, who after the 1905 Revolution had begun to find a political voice in the State Duma, provided a source of patronage for the new art. They commissioned modern buildings by such architects as Shekhtel; sponsored the Symbolist painters of the Blue Rose group and their successors; and introduced Russia to the latest developments in French art by throwing open their extensive private collections to the public. Works by Van Gogh and Gauguin as well as the newest paintings by Picasso and Matisse were seen in the Moscow collections of Ivan Morozov and Sergei Shchukhin. The radical nature of this work provided a vital stimulus to a rising generation of young Russian artists.

Modern art movements which had been separated by generations in the West swept into Russia in the space of a decade: Impressionism, Symbolism, Post-Impressionism, Cubism and Fauvism were all adapted; faction followed faction, theories bred counter-theories, artistic reality became governed by its own aesthetic and pictorial laws. The Futurists anticipated the apocalyptic release of society's headlong lurch towards self-destruction in their paintings and performances. Desire became fact in Russia's vainglorious and inept engagement in the First World War – the deathwish of a bankrupt society.

'The Battle Song of the Russian Sailors', 1904 – a Russian propaganda postcard showing the Baltic fleet, which had recently been deployed in the Far East, trouncing the Japanese.

Japanese woodblock print showing the destruction of the Baltic fleet by the Japanese navy off Tsushima, May 1905. This humiliating and costly defeat forced the Russian Emperor to sue for peace.

Desecrated Torah scrolls in the synagogue at Kishinev after the pogrom, 1903.

During 1903 social and political stability began to deteriorate rapidly as a wave of strikes spread across the country; these were brutally suppressed by Tsarist troops. Inspired by the idea of a mystical, Orthodox crusade, the Tsarist-backed Union of Russian People sponsored the Black Hundreds in their provocation of 'enemies of autocracy' and in their inhuman pogroms against the Jews. In opposition to this, the movement for reform gathered strength. When, in January 1905, troops opened fire on a peaceful demonstration, killing over two hundred people on a day which came to be known as Bloody Sunday, a general strike was called amid an atmosphere of international outrage.

A band of Black Hundreds march through Moscow with the banner of the Tsar, November 1905.

Political meeting of factory workers in Briansk, October 1905.

Cover design by Boris Kustodiev ▶ for the short-lived satirical magazine *Red Laughter*, to commemorate the first anniversary of Bloody Sunday.

Ilya Repin, *17 October 1905*, 1911.

Konstantin Pobedonotsev, Procurator of the Holy Synod from 1880 to 1905, believed that 'parliaments are the great lie of our time' and that autocracy was the only possible basis for government in Russia. His ideas greatly influenced the political outlook of Tsars Alexander III and Nicholas II, until he resigned from his post in the aftermath of Bloody Sunday.

In the Manifesto of 17 October 1905 the Tsar was forced to concede various constitutional reforms, but their spirit was never fully implemented. The 1905 cartoon 'The House of Cards, Our Constitution. Please Don't Blow' symbolizes the attempts of Count Witte, the new Prime Minister, to carry out reform. The Tsar's concessions effectively split the opposition, with the moderates optimistic of improvement.

Six years later Ilya Repin captured the elation of the time in his painting *17 October 1905*; but there are presages of the future in the tense, mask-like expressions of the demonstrators. After October the Workers' Soviet alone continued to resist the authorities and Christmas 1905 was marked by savage street fighting in the poorer districts of Moscow. Isaac Brodsky's painting *Red Funeral* (1906) shows the aftermath of the suppression of such revolts.

Isaac Brodsky, *Red Funeral*, 1906. ▶

'The House of Cards', 1905.

Repin, *Portrait of Konstantin Pobedonotsev*, 1901-3.

49

Kasimir Malevich,
Woman in Childbirth, 1908.

Victor Borisov-Musatov,
Sleep of the Gods, 1903.

Kuzma Petrov-Vodkin,
***The Red Horse*, 1912.**

The banner of Modernism, borne in St Petersburg by the World of Art group, was taken up by the Symbolists using such French painters as Puvis de Chavannes and Maurice Denis as models. This can be sensed in the attenuated line and close colour harmonies of Victor Borisov-Musatov's *Self-Portrait with Sister* (1898) and *Sleep of the Gods* (1903).

Borisov-Musatov died in 1905 yet his work provided an inspiration for the Blue Rose, a younger group of artists comprising Pavel Kuznetsov, Nikolai Sapunov and Martiros Saryan, whose 1907 Moscow exhibition was backed by Nikolai Ryabushinsky, banker and publisher of *The Golden Fleece,* a Moscow-based Symbolist artistic review.

The intense colours of Gauguin were adopted by Kasimir Malevich, Ivan Kliun and Kuzma Petrov-Vodkin in such overtly Symbolist paintings as *Woman in Childbirth* (1908), *Consumption, Portrait of the Artist's Wife* (1910) and *The Red Horse* (1912). The spirituality and heightened colour of such paintings were a first step in the subsequent move towards non-objectivity.

Ivan Kliun, *Consumption,*
***Portrait of the Artist's Wife*, 1910.**

Victor Borisov-Musatov,
***Self Portrait with Sister*, 1898.**

51

Alexander Scriabin with his wife Tatiana and son Julian, 1913.

Valery Briussov was one of the protagonists of Russian literary decadence and editor of *The Scales,* a Symbolist review which published Western poems in translation as well as new work by Russian writers. Much of Briussov's work had a strongly apocalyptic tone and his poem *The Coming of the Huns* (1903) prophetically welcomed the destructive power of the Mongol hordes. Alexander Blok's at first more intimate lyrical Symbolism had by 1906 become cynical and disillusioned; a mood of hopelessness and depression pervaded his writings until the Revolution of 1917. His poem *On Kulikovo Field* (1908) refers to the Russian victory over the Mongols in the fourteenth century yet also seems to predict the impending destruction of the First World War.

Between 1906 and 1908 Vsevolod Meyerhold produced three of Blok's Symbolist dramas – *The Puppet Show, The King in the Square* and *The Stranger.* A protégé of Stanislavsky, Meyerhold had moved to Vera Komissarzhevskaya's St Petersburg theatre where he perfected an ironic, anti-naturalist, Symbolist theatre based on parody and mime.

Musicians were also influenced by Symbolism: Sergei Rachmaninov's *The Isle of the Dead* (1909) was an interpretation of the famous painting by Arnold Böcklin. Alexander Scriabin's *Poem of Ecstasy* (1907) manifests a more joyous pantheism; at this time Scriabin was pursuing his researches in synaesthesia, in which the stimulation of one sense echoes in another. For him sound and colour were linked and, accordingly, he began to provide colour notes for his scores and constructed a colour organ which could play this music.

Alexander Blok, c. 1906.

◄ **Boris Grigoriev,** *Double Portrait of Vsevolod Meyerhold,* **1916.**

Mikhail Vrubel, *Portrait of Valery Briussov,* **1906.**

In 1906 Serge Diaghilev first broke away from the restricting confines of the Russian art world to work in Paris. He began to channel his energies into the promotion of Russian art, opera and ballet abroad and in 1909 presented the first season of the Ballets Russes. Within a short time these colourful and lavish productions had achieved great popularity and became synonymous in the West with an exotic view of Russia which reflected the passions of ancient fairy tales. Diaghilev hand-picked composers and artists to work together in an opulent harmony: old friends from St Petersburg such as Bakst, Benois and Bilibin worked alongside such leading artists as Picasso, Matisse and Cocteau. The dancers Tamara Karsavina and Vaslav Nijinsky and the choreographer Mikhail Fokine became strongly identified with the Ballets Russes, as did the young Igor Stravinsky whose specially commissioned ballets *Firebird* (1910), *Petrushka* (1911) and *The Rite of Spring* (1913) became a vital part of the Diaghilev repertoire. The second phase of the Ballets Russes, departing from *The Rite of Spring,* broke away from exoticism to establish new forms of artistic co-operation with leading avant-garde artists, choreographers and musicians.

'St Petersburg at Night', a curtain design by Alexander Benois for Stravinsky's ballet *Petrushka*, 1911.

Tamara Karsavina in the title role of Stravinsky's *Firebird*, 1910. Costume by Leon Bakst. Photo by E. O. Hoppé.

◀ **In permanent exile from the land of their inspiration, Diaghilev and the Ballets Russes leave Chicago during their successful 1916 American tour. *From left to right:* Adolph Bolm, Serge Grigoriev, Leonid Massine, Lydia Sokolova, Hilda Buick, Diaghilev, Lydia Lopokova, Liubov Tenisheva, Olga Kokhlova and Nicola Kreusnef.**

Scene from Stravinsky's *The Rite of Spring*, 1913. Costumes by Nikolai Roerich.

Matisse, *The Dance*, 1910, commissioned by Shchukhin.

The Picasso Room in the Trubetskoy Palace,
Sergei Shchukhin's Moscow house.

Feodor Shekhtel, Utro Rossii Printing House, Moscow 1907. ▶

Valentin Serov, *Portrait of Mikhail Morozov*, 1902.

Feodor Shekhtel, main staircase,
Stepan Ryabushinsky's house,
Moscow 1900-2.

Feodor Shekhtel, the Ryabushinsky
bank, Moscow 1904.
The upper storey, designed by
I. S. Kuznetsov, was added in 1908.

The rapid development of modern art and architecture depended upon the patronage of a handful of rich Moscow merchant families. Mikhail Morozov, painted by Valentin Serov in 1902, was a member of a rich textile family; he collected French paintings, especially Degas and Gauguin, and his brother Ivan subsequently built up a large collection of works by Matisse and Picasso. Sergei was the most eminent collector of another established Moscow merchant family, the Shchukhins. His home, the eighteenth-century Trubetskoy Palace in which whole rooms were devoted to the work of Matisse and Picasso, was opened to the public on special days so that they could inspect the latest purchases. The Ryabushinsky family had widespread interests in industry, banking and the stock exchange. Nikolai was an active patron of the arts and Stepan commissioned an Art Nouveau mansion (1900-2) from Feodor Shekhtel, who had already completed a number of major new buildings for the Morozovs. In 1902 Shekhtel was asked by Pavel and Vladimir Ryabushinsky to provide a facelift to an old building in which they had installed the new Ryabushinsky bank. The white glazed brick piers of the stark façade were a model for Shekhtel's next major commission, the Utro Rossii Printing House (1907) where Pavel Ryabushinsky's progressive newspaper *The Morning of Russia* was published. During 1911 the newspaper was temporarily closed on the Tsar's orders for attacking the government.

57

Vladimir Tatlin, *Self Portrait*, **1910.**

Natalia Goncharova, *Selling Bread*, **1911.**

Niko Pirosmani,
The Feast of the Five Princes, c. 1909.

Kasimir Malevich, *The Bather*, **1910.**

The aestheticism and decadence of the Symbolists were felt by many younger artists to be the death rattle of a dying culture. Consciously turning away from St Petersburg and the West they looked for renewal in the arts, crafts and icons of ancient Russia as well as in the art of children, peasants and primitive painters, such as the Georgian Niko Pirosmani. The first manifestations of this neo-primitivism were shown in the Moscow Association of Artists Exhibition of April 1907, to which Natalia Goncharova, Mikhail Larionov, Kasimir Malevich and Georgy Yakulov all contributed work.

◀ **Mikhail Larionov,** *Spring*, **1912.**

Malevich, *Head of a Peasant Girl*, 1913.

Goncharova and Larionov with painted motifs on their faces in a scene from the film *Drama in Cabaret 13*, 1914.

Photo of the Futurist poet and theorist of *zaum*, Velimir Khlebnikov, with daughter of a wine merchant, c. 1910.

Pavel Filonov, *Man and Woman*, 1912.

Primitivism provided the spring-board for further abstraction. Although still loosely representational, Larionov and Goncharova tried in their Rayonist paintings to express the spiritual essence of their subjects in order to erode the barrier between art and life. Similar concerns preoccupied the Futurist painters and poets who in their work and iconoclastic performances repudiated previous art and reflected the arbitrariness of modern reality in *zaum* (transsense) – a new form of logic which transcended conventional language. In the Moscow Exhibition of Painting in 1915 Rayonism was over-shadowed by the more audacious experiments of the Futurists.

The influence of Picasso can be seen clearly in Malevich's *Head of a Peasant Girl* (1913), and the spatial planes of Cubism and the alogical elements of Futurism are combined in his *An Englishman in Moscow* (1914). These tendencies were combined in Russia into a new movement – Cubo-Futurism.

Malevich, *An Englishman in Moscow*, 1914.

Natalia Goncharova, *Yellow and Green Forest*, a Rayonist painting of c. 1912.

Tatlin, Udaltsova, V. Pestel, V. Prudkovskaya and an unidentified girl waiting at Vlakhernskaya station on the Savelovsk railway-line, summer 1915.

Poster for 0.10 The Last Futurist Painting Exhibition, Petrograd 1915.

Installation of paintings by Malevich at the 0.10 exhibition.

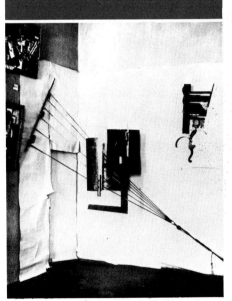

One of Tatlin's counter-reliefs at the 0.10 exhibition.

0.10

At 0.10 The Last Futurist Painting Exhibition, organized by Ivan Puni in Petrograd during the winter of 1915-16, the two most advanced tendencies in Russian art came face to face. Malevich exhibited thirty-six non-objective Suprematist paintings for the first time along with a manifesto stating his intentions. For Malevich Suprematism was 'the zero of form ... [which] untied the knots of wisdom and liberated the consciousness of colour.'

Malevich's search for the cosmic was not shared by Vladimir Tatlin who, repudiating what he regarded as amateurism, refused to share a gallery with such work and set up a separate section for his counter-reliefs along with paintings by Liubov Popova and Nadezhda Udaltsova. Tatlin's reliefs were built up in the manner of three-dimensional paintings with an emphasis on the diverse materials out of which they were constructed. The leaflet Tatlin produced to mark the exhibition was factual and unpretentious. There was no explanation of the work or attempt at theory.

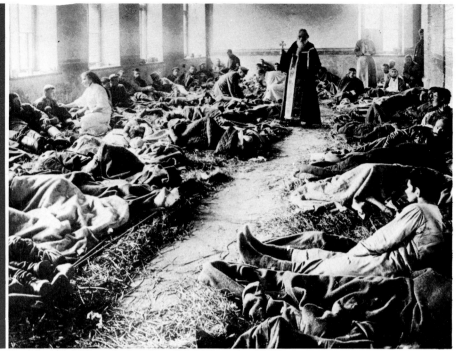

Russian field hospital at Suvalki, Lithuania, 1915.

When war was declared in August 1914 many artists rallied to the cause of Russia as protector of fellow-Slavs in the Balkans. In propaganda posters the Tsar posed as the champion of 'Freedom, Truth and Right' in a crusade by Holy Russia against the forces of darkness and repression. The German army was accused of atrocities: the indiscriminate slaughter of non-combatants, women and children. Such propaganda enabled the strong blood relations between the Tsarist and German Imperial households to be completely overlooked. However, successive defeats, high casualties, poor supply lines, the isolation of the Emperor and his household and the food crisis of 1917 demoralized both the army and the public at large. Many questioned the Emperor's ability to govern and chauvinist belligerence began to be replaced by an overwhelming desire for peace.

Surrender of the Russian army at Tannenburg, 1917.

'The Tired Soldier' — anti-war poster by Leonid Pasternak for the Petrograd Soviet of Workers' and Soldiers' Deputies, 1917.

Captured Russian soldiers, September 1915.

Poster showing Kaiser Wilhelm as ▶ 'The German Antichrist', c. 1915.

The Bolsheviks seize power

Soldiers deserting from the First World War swelled the Bolshevik ranks and Lenin's call for 'Peace, Bread and Land' appealed to the masses; the support of these groups enabled the Bolsheviks to seize power in October 1917, and the new government made peace with Germany at Brest-Litovsk in March 1918. But by the summer of 1918 Counter-Revolutionary (White) forces had mobilized and an attempt was made on Lenin's life. The Bolsheviks responded with mass arrests and executions, and with the suppression of virtually all non-Bolshevik newspapers. The Civil War between the Reds and the Whites lasted until November 1920.

The new Soviet state fought the Whites on every level, orchestrating a brilliant propaganda campaign using posters, cartoons, theatrical sketches and films to inform the mostly illiterate masses of the benefits of the new régime and of the dangers and penalties of collaboration. At the outbreak of the Revolution few artists rallied to the cause: Mayakovsky, Meyerhold and Blok were among the first to declare their support. Mayakovsky and his friends printed the large stencilled Rosta posters which were run off and distributed to public buildings throughout the Republic. Using the simple language of the cartoon, these were an important political influence providing information about public health, safety at work and literacy campaigns, as well as about the exploitation of workers and peasants under capitalism. Anatoly Lunacharsky, People's Commissar for Enlightenment, enlisted the help of many more artists and writers in the battle for hearts and minds, and their message was taken to all corners of the Republic by specially decorated 'agit' (agitational) trains and boats.

Lenin and Lunacharsky were quick to suppress the artistic iconoclasm of the Proletkult (Proletarian Culture) groups and to safeguard works of art and public monuments. The directorate and staff in the main art galleries and museums in Moscow and Petrograd remained unchanged. Some artists, however, reserved their support and waited to see what would happen. Maxim Gorky's Vsermirnaia (Universal) publishing house provided a focus for writers who did not immediately subscribe to Marxism. A few intellectuals left the country to swell the already large communities of Russian emigrés in Paris and Berlin – refugees from the previous régime.

Yet overall the Revolution was a stimulus to the production of art. By breaking down old modes of representation and in their search for utopias, many abstract artists had felt that they were harbingers of the Revolution. After October 1917 a period of frenetic experimentation accompanied a detailed examination of the vocabulary of form and colour. Malevich dematerialized the subject itself in pictures made with white paint on a white background; Rodchenko and others analyzed the elements of line, colour, mass and surface in painting and sculpture in logical series. But such work was only of limited public appeal – it was Revolutionary by analogy, through its formal innovation rather than through what it depicted. By 1921 non-objective painting had reached a crisis of confidence and could not transcend further limits – alternatives had to be found.

'Death, the Reaper' – anti-war Revolutionary hoardings, Petrograd 1917.

At the front morale was low: five Russian soldiers died for every German they killed; desertions were widespread and increased dramatically after the collapse of the Galician offensive in July 1917. This demonstration of soldiers and workers in Petrograd during 1917 shows the widespread popular support for the Bolshevik peace programme. The banners proclaim: 'Long Live the Democratic Republic', 'Land and Freedom' and 'Down with the Old World

Postcard of Lenin by B. Yemirov, 1918.

Cover of *The Communist International*, published in Moscow, May 1919.

ПЕРВОЕ МАЯ ПЕРВОЕ
МЕЖДУНАРОДНЫЙ ПРАЗДНИК ТРУДА.

1889 – 1919

May Day poster commemorating an international festival of labour, 1919.

The People's Militia, Petrograd 1917.

The October Revolution was engineered by both Lenin and Trotsky in a virtually bloodless coup on 24 and 25 October 1917. The cruiser Aurora fired blank shells at the Winter Palace to intimidate the Provisional Government, which subsequently surrendered without a struggle. One consequence was the formation of the new People's Militia, which kept the cities running. Another was that, as the apparatus of the Tsarist Empire began to be dismantled, women were given equal rights.

Leon Trotsky, 1918.
Photo by Moisei Nappelbaum.

NEW DIRECTION

Lunacharsky inspects the V. I. Lenin agit train, Moscow 1919. ▼ An agit ship, c. 1920.

The V.I. Lenin agit train stops off in the countryside, 1920. The slogan to the right of the entrance reads: 'The Sun of the Soviet Republic illuminates the path of truth, knowledge and right. THOSE WHO KNOW THIS, SO WILL THEY TRIUMPH.'

On 26 October 1917 the Bolshevik Central Committee announced the members of Lenin's government: Anatoly Lunacharsky was to be head of the People's Commissariat for Enlightenment (Narkompros). A writer and critic, he described himself as 'an intellectual among Bolsheviks and a Bolshevik among intellectuals', and as head of Narkompros he was a committed supporter of the widespread dissemination of the arts. In the early days after the Revolution he organized a programme for the erection of new monuments, most of them temporary structures, and gave support and patronage to avant-garde as well as traditional artists.

Before the days of radio, agit trains and ships played a valuable role in widely disseminating information and propaganda during the Civil War, using leaflets, film and 'Theatre of the People'. Mass public spectacles were staged, such as the open-air re-enactment of the October Revolution in Petrograd in 1920. It included over 8000 actors and was directed by Nikolai Evreinov, a pupil of Vera Kommissarshevskaya before the war and a devotee of Aubrey Beardsley and Oscar Wilde; now he became the protagonist of the idea of 'synthetic theatre'.

The agit film *Red Imps* (1923), directed by Ivan Perestani and produced by the film section of the Georgian Commissariat of Enlightenment, was a spectacular and popular adventure story of young people acting as scouts for Budyonny's Red Cavalry against the Whites, during the Civil War.

Propaganda leaflets being unloaded from an agit train, c. 1920. Painted on the sliding door are the front pages and titles of the leading Bolshevik newspapers.

Scene from Ivan Perestani's *Red Imps*, 1923.

Open-air re-enactment of the October Revolution, Petrograd, 1920.

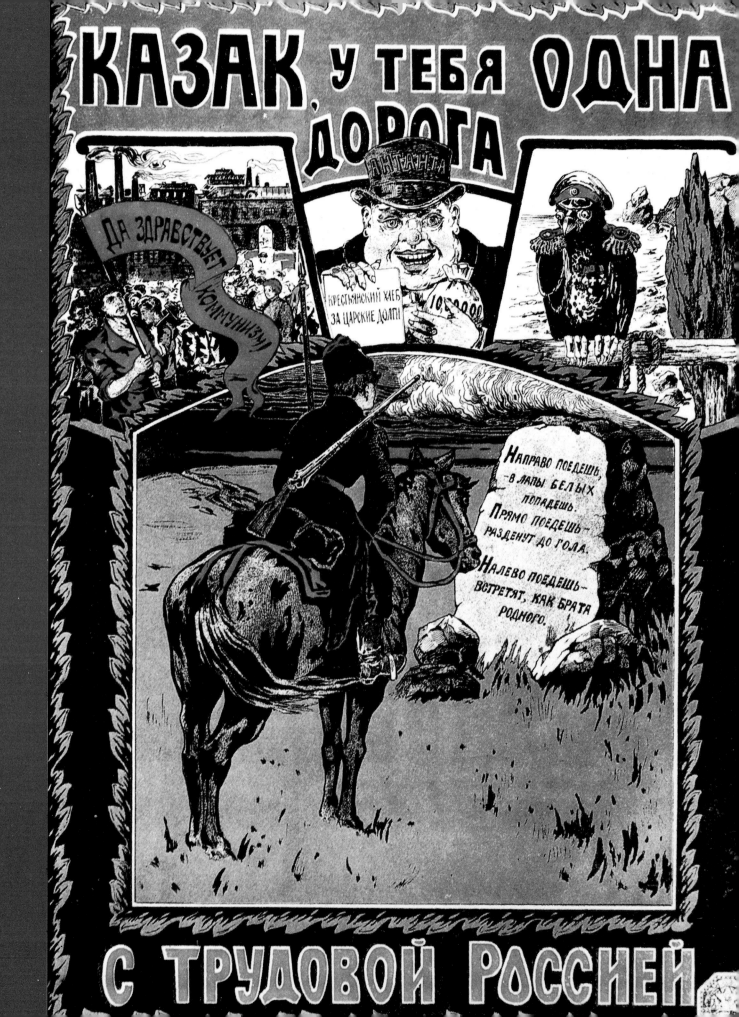

During the Civil War 1917-20 many leading artists and writers devoted their talents to the production of propaganda in support of the Bolshevik government.

'Icon painter' Victor Deni parodies the traditional icon of the Holy Mother of Sellansk, showing the White leader Chernov holding Admiral Kolchak who has in his hand the notice: 'Every tenth worker and peasant will be shot.' Generals Yudenich and Denikin are attendant angels. c. 1920.

Dmitri Moor, 'Early sang the little birds as they did not fear the little cat', 1919. Generals Denikin and Yudenich are throttled by the hands of the Dictatorship of the Proletariat.

◀ Dmitri Moor, 'Cossack your only way is with Workers' Russia', 1920. The motif is taken from Vasnetsov's painting *Knight at the Crossroads* (see p.30).

Viktor Deni, 'Start Moving in Time', 1920. The Polish landlords and General Wrangel are decapitated by a Russian peasant.

'The Revolution calls everyone to try ▶ harder at work' says the slogan printed above production statistics.

Decorations for Red Square, c. 1920.

In the first years after the Revolution, when building materials were in short supply, artists and architects turned their attention towards temporary structures which could be made easily and cheaply, and which conveyed a simple propaganda message. The forms of these structures expressed their meaning, as in the design for a public rostrum based on the hammer and sickle, made by an unknown Proletkult artist in about 1920.

At the start of the New Economic Policy, the Government began to release information about the construction of Soviet industry and the need to build it up against the encroachment of private enterprise. For the 1921 May Day celebrations, painted propaganda panels were erected in Sverdlov Square in Moscow which stressed the need to work hard to get Soviet industry back on its feet.

Timber production 'strengthens the ▶ union between town and country' and **'the forest is our wealth'** are the slogans which surround the statistics of production and export over the previous two years.

Public rostrum, c. 1920.

Opposite page: **Steel production in the Donbas (Don Basin): 'the heart of Russia'** is encouraged, with **'hammer and drill in hand'**, to march into production with **'the energy of ten'.**

Marc Chagall, *En avant,* **gouache, 1917.** ▼ **Chagall teaching war orphans at the Malachovka Colony, Vitebsk** *c.* **1918.**

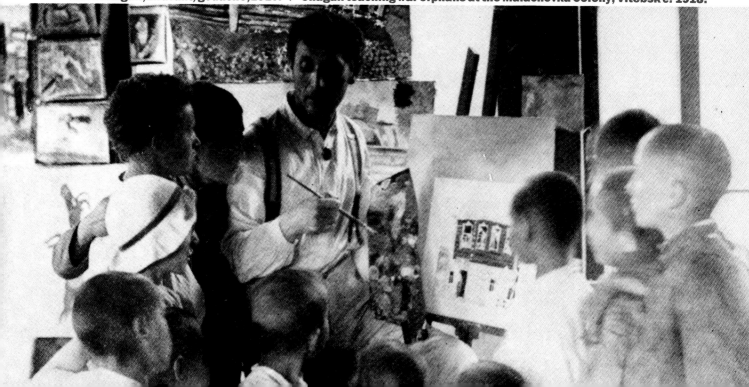

El Lissitzky in his studio, Vitebsk 1919.

Unovis agit-poster in a Vitebsk street, 1919. The text reads: 'The machine tools of the depots, factories and plants are awaiting you.'

Malevich, Lissitzky and other members of Unovis board the train to leave Vitebsk for Moscow in 1921.

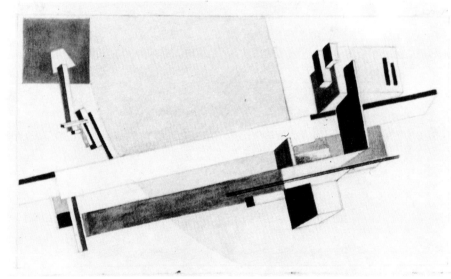

El Lissitzky, *Proun, Bridge 1*, 1919.

In 1918 Marc Chagall was appointed Director of the Free Art Studios in his home town of Vitebsk, and El Lissitzky joined him as a teacher of architecture and graphics. The following year Malevich was invited by Chagall to teach at the school, and he soon attracted a group of young disciples who called themselves Unovis – the Champions of the New Art. They enthusiastically adopted the tenets of Suprematism, not only in painting but also in street propaganda, architecture, decorative schemes and applied arts. Chagall returned from an extended trip to Moscow to find Malevich in charge of the school; there was a confrontation and Chagall subsequently resigned. In 1921 Malevich left Vitebsk for Moscow along with many of the Unovis group.

Inkhuk, the Institute of Artistic Culture, was formed in May 1920 in Moscow to provide a forum for various investigations into the theory and practice of art. Vassily Kandinsky was the first director and under his influence the Institute concentrated on the synthetic, intuitive and psychological aspects of creativity. This led to friction with colleagues such as Rodchenko and to Kandinsky's leaving the Institute at the end of the year to return to Germany.

In 1920 Rodchenko began to make three-dimensional constructions composed of elements of the same size: constructions which were exhibited, along with the work of other Constructivists, at the Obmokhu (Society of Young Artists) second exhibition in Moscow in May 1921. At the same time he was experimenting with similarly impersonal line and circle motifs in his paintings.

Naum Gabo had, independently, from 1916 been combining naturalism with monumentality, using the materials and techniques of engineering. His intentions were codified in August 1920 in *The Realistic Manifesto,* which he published with his brother Antoine Pevsner. In this they put forward the ideal of a new non-referential rhythmical Constructivism.

Vassily Kandinsky, *Untitled (Red Square)*, 1917.

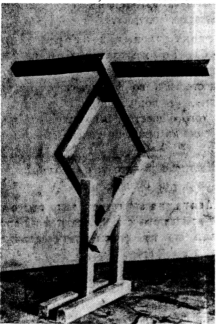

**Alexander Rodchenko,
Wooden Construction, 1920.**

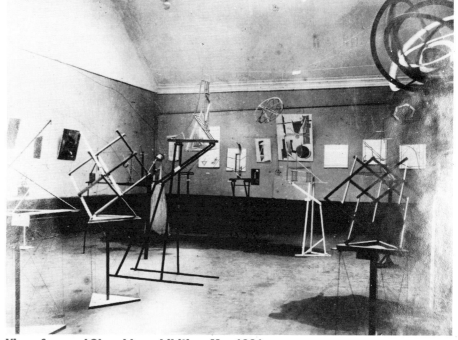

View of second Obmokhu exhibition, May 1921.

Naum Gabo, Constructed Head No.2, 1916. ▶

At the beginning of 1921 Inkhuk was re-organized by Rodchenko with Stepanova, the sculptor Alexei Babichev and the musician Nadezhda Briusova. Babichev drew up a plan for the analysis of the 'culture of materials' and the vocabulary of form based on rational laboratory principles.

In September, under the auspices of Inkhuk in an exhibition entitled 5x5=25, the end of non-functional experimental abstract art was effectively spelled out. Five artists – Exter, Popova, Rodchenko, Stepanova and Vesnin – each submitted five works. Rodchenko showed three monochrome canvases in red, yellow and blue; these were the logical conclusion to his researches of the previous four years.

At a meeting of Inkhuk late in November the majority of the group dissociated themselves from easel painting and advocated in its place 'the absoluteness of industrial art and Constructivism'.

El Lissitzky, cover for *Veshch* (*Object*), an international art magazine, published in Berlin by Inkhuk, 1922.

Alexander Vesnin, cover for catalogue of 5x5=25, 1921.

Alexander Rodchenko, poster design for 5x5=25, 1921.

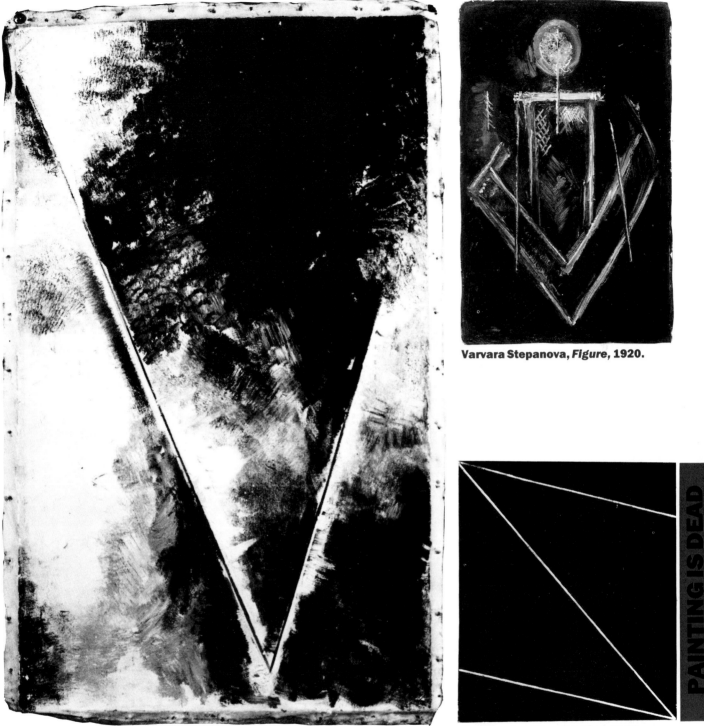

Varvara Stepanova, *Figure*, 1920.

Rodchenko, *Line Painting*, 1920.

Alexander Rodchenko, *The Dissolution of the Surface*, 1920.

A NEW WORLD

Cultural energy during the New Economic Policy

1921-28

After the dislocation of the Civil War and the terrible Volga famine of 1921, the securing of reliable food supplies was a major priority for Lenin's government. The New Economic Policy was born of expediency in an attempt to stimulate agricultural and industrial production by re-introducing private enterprise. Goods produced by state industries had to compete with those privately produced, hence the advertising campaign developed by artist-constructor Alexander Rodchenko and poet-copywriter Vladimir Mayakovsky in favour of state stores (*Gum* and *Mosselprom*), using eye-catching slogans and amusing verses to stimulate demand.

Radical artists now began to fulfil the prophecies of the Futurists by moving away from the pre-Revolutionary idea that art is separate from life, to work on the design and decoration of functional objects which could be mass-produced by state industries. Production art, as this movement became known, centred on a group of artists and writers who worked first for Inkhuk (the Institute of Artistic Culture) and later on the magazine *LEF*.

In 1923 Varvara Stepanova and Liubov Popova, two members of the LEF (Left Front of the Arts) group, began to work as consultant designers for the First Moscow Textile Mill. They, and other artists such as Alexandra Exter, Vladimir Tatlin and Vera Mukhina, also began to design clothes for mass production.

In Leningrad, Ilya Chasnik and Nikolai Suetin, former pupils of Malevich and members of Ginkhuk (the Leningrad Institute of Artistic Culture), adapted Suprematist designs to the fine ceramics produced by the State Porcelain Factory in an attempt to establish a universal decorative harmony. Most of their work was intended for the luxury export market but some items were mass-produced by other factories for the home market.

Artists and architects planned new forms of buildings: Malevich worked on a rhythmical system of floating skyscrapers, which could never be realized; Ginsburg and the OSA (Union of Contemporary Architecture) group of avant-garde Moscow architects developed advanced designs for communal living in new apartment blocks; while Melnikov, Golossov and the Vesnin brothers designed workers' clubs — vast complexes to serve the recreational, educational and health needs of large communities and factories.

In all the arts there was a search for new forms to express the new realities of Soviet life, and an energy of innovation was characteristic. Not everyone, however, shared this enthusiasm; there was a feeling that such experiments, although well-meaning ideologically, could not be understood by the masses. The preserve of the intelligentsia, this art had no proletarian credentials. Neither Lenin nor Lunacharsky, the Commissar for Public Enlightenment, had believed in the creation of a new proletarian art but had preferred to retain and build on the best of the old; this allowed for a diversity of culture. When their influence waned, previous options were closed and a new monolithic order began to be imposed.

Documentary film-maker Dziga Vertov, c. 1922.

Still from Vertov's *Kino Pravda* newsreel
on the Volga famine, 1921.

Agriculture gets back on its feet with help from the army.
In the absence of a tractor, a captured British tank is used to till
the ground, autumn 1922.

Konstantin Yuon, *The New Planet*, 1921. ▼ Isaac Brodsky, *The Shooting of the 26 Baku Commissars*, 1925.

Kliment Redko, *Uprising*, 1923-5. This painting shows the Soviet leadership before Trotsky's exile.

Solomon Nikritin, *Farewell to the Dead*, 1926.

Avant-garde abstract art, even at its height, had never supplanted the mainstream of realism which ran uninterrupted from the Wanderers. During the 1920s a number of realist artists' groups were founded, the most influential and conservative of which was the AKhRR (The Association of Artists of Revolutionary Russia). During the 1920s a younger generation of painters, such as Kliment Redko, Solomon Nikritin and Alexander Drevin, moved away from literal depiction towards an expressive and symbolic realism.

General Budyonny at the opening of the AKhRR exhibition to celebrate ten years of the Red Army, 1928. On the left is the artist E. Katsman; on the right, F. Bogorodsky.

89

The turbulent decades before and after the Revolution were a high point of lyrical poetry.

Anna Akhmatova, Boris Pasternak and Sergei Esenin all eschewed a public function for their art in favour of an exploration of their subjective and emotional lives. As a result of her marriage with poet and Counter-Revolutionary Nikolai Gumilov, who was shot by the Bolsheviks in 1921, Akhmatova did not find favour with the authorities. Esenin, the lyric poet of the Russian countryside, hanged himself in a Leningrad hotel room in 1925. Pasternak was at first associated with the LEF group but during the 1920s he gravitated away from its rational functionalism towards an intense and personal imagery.

Anna Akhmatova, 1924. Photo by Moisei Nappelbaum, a leading portrait photographer in the 1920s and 30s.

Boris Pasternak, 1914.

Sergei Esenin (left) with poet and writer Sergei Gorodetsky, Petrograd 1915.

◀ **Nathan Altman, *Portrait of Anna Akhmatova*, 1914.**

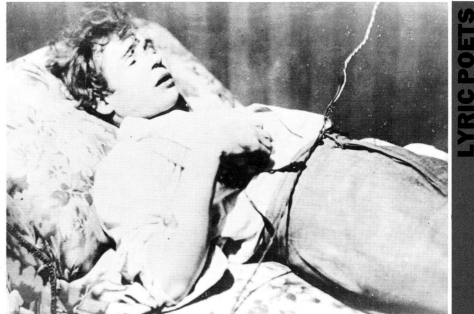

Sergei Esenin a few hours after his death, 28 December 1925, Leningrad.

From 1922, in response to pressure from Inkhuk, the Constructivists moved away from subjective experiment to become more closely involved in functional design, as well as in photography and architecture. As designers at the First Moscow Textile Mill, Varvara Stepanova and Liubov Popova chose motifs based on rational geometric principles – some abstract, some representational, as in Popova's small repeat pattern of a hammer and sickle. Working in Petrograd/Leningrad the Suprematists were also concerned to impose their system onto architectural and industrial design. Luxury industries such as the State (formerly Imperial) Porcelain factory had to serve the people by producing either sumptuously crafted propaganda for export or new forms for popular use.

Mikhail Adamovich, *The Red Star*, plate, 1922.

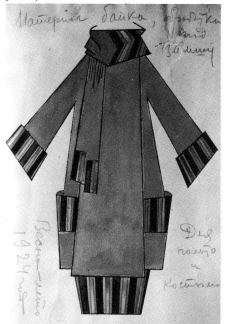

Liubov Popova, overcoat design, 1924.

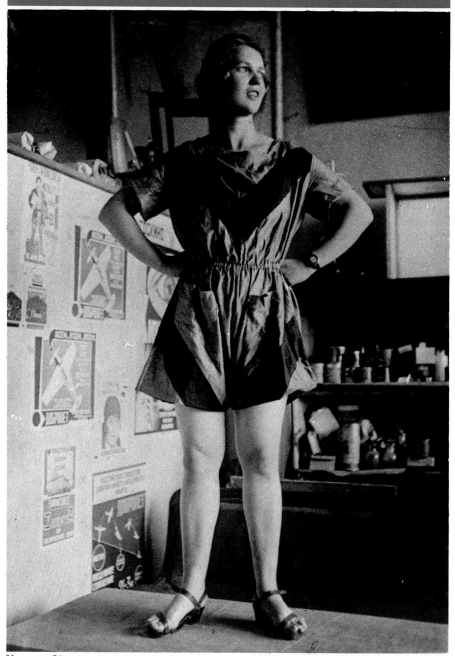

Varvara Stepanova, women's sports clothes, 1924.

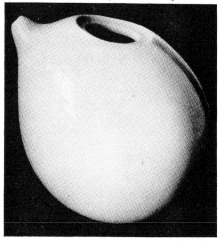

A. G. Sotnikov, teapot, 1930. Sotnikov was a pupil of Tatlin.

Kasimir Malevich, teapot, 1923.

Varvara Stepanova wearing
a dress of her own design, 1924.
Photo by Rodchenko.

Agitational porcelain from the State Porcelain factory, Petrograd, 1922.

НОВЫЙ БЫТ

Vladimir Tatlin wearing an overcoat of
his own design, 1924.

Engravers at the State Porcelain
factory, Petrograd, c. 1922.

Nikolai Suetin, Suprematist vase, 1923.

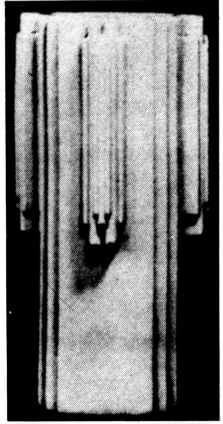

Rodchenko, photomontage for cover of *LEF* no. 2, 1923.

LEF was a group of artists centred around the journal edited by Osip Brik and Vladimir Mayakovsky. Influential members of the group included the artist-constructors Alexander Rodchenko, Varvara Stepanova and Anton Lavinsky; the film-makers Dziga Vertov and Sergei Eisenstein; and the writers Sergei Tretiakov, Nikolai Aseev, Victor Shklovsky and Semeon Kirsanov. Published between 1923 and 1925 and revived as *Novy LEF* during 1927 and 1928 under the editorship of Mayakovsky and Tretiakov, the journal provided a valuable forum for advanced aesthetics, particularly concentrating on the question of the responsibility of the artist to society and his or her role in it as animator and designer.

Editorial meeting of *Novy LEF*, c. 1927. Osip Brik in the chair, Mayakovsky to his right, Rodchenko to his left.

Nikolai Aseev, 1927. Photo by Rodchenko.

◀ **Lily Brik, 1924. Photo by Rodchenko.**   **Anton Lavinsky, 1924. Photo by Rodchenko.**

The decade saw a dramatic expansion in the number of theatres in the USSR, both avant-garde and traditional. In the autumn of 1921 Vsevolod Meyerhold moved from the RSFSR Theatre No. 1 to be the Director of the new State Higher Theatre Workshop in Moscow. His work there completely rejected the refined Symbolist aesthetic of his past, which was replaced by Revolutionary forms and repertoire. On May Day 1921 he staged an updated version of Mayakovsky's agit-play *Mystery Bouffe,* in which the proscenium arch was dispensed with for the first time and the flat stage replaced by a series of different levels; there was no front curtain or flown scenery. This design was an important break from past tradition and set the pattern for subsequent developments in Constructivist stage design. Over the next two years Meyerhold collaborated with Liubov Popova and Varvara Stepanova who designed impersonal machine-like sets and costumes which the actors, whom Meyerhold trained to move like machines themselves, could operate. Baron Nikolai Foregger in his MASTFOR studio and Alexander Tairov at the Kamerny Theatre also experimented with the mechanical forms of Constructivism. Together their productions achieved a balance of association and visual effect which totally repudiated the theatrical realism of Stanislavsky.

At the Petrograd Museum of Artistic Culture Tatlin began to turn his attention to stage design. For a memorial performance of Velimir Khlebnikov's dramatic poem *Zangezi* (1923) in which he himself participated, he constructed a vast counter-relief in which the actors could sit or stand.

Anton Lavinsky's set for Mayakovsky's *Mystery-Bouffe,* 1921.

Vladimir Tatlin's stage design for Khlebnikov's *Zangezi* at the Petrograd Museum of Artistic Culture, 1923.

Liubov Popova's stage design for Crommelynck's *The Magnanimous Cuckold,* 1922, at the new Actors' Theatre in Moscow.

◀ **Vsevolod Meyerhold, 1923.**

Baron Nikolai Foregger, *c.* 1923.

97

Both the future and the past were depicted by artists in the new mechanized Constructivist style. Alexander Tairov pioneered a spare, expressive style of acting supplemented by mime and acrobatics. Yet in 1922 these experiments were soon surpassed by Meyerhold's new productions of *The Magnanimous Cuckold* and *Tarelkin's Death,* designed by Popova and Stepanova; the young Sergei Eisenstein, fresh from MASTFOR, worked as artistic director on *Tarelkin's Death.* In March 1923 Popova designed Tretiakov's *The Earth in Turmoil* for Meyerhold, in which a car, motorcycles, field telephones, machine guns, a mobile army kitchen and a combine harvester were all introduced as props.

The novel *Aelita* (1922) by Alexei Tostoy, and the 1924 film based on it were both extremely popular. The plot told of a Soviet expedition to Mars, which resulted in a love affair between a Russian engineer and a Martian woman, and the attempted overthrow of the oppressive Martian social hierarchy. The costumes were designed by Alexandra Exter and the sets were by Isaac Rabinovich and Victor Simov.

Still from *Aelita*, 1924.

Alisa Koonen playing the title role in Tairov's production of Racine's *Phaedre* in the Kamerny Theatre, Moscow 1921. The costume was designed by Georgy Stenberg.

◀ **Still from the science-fiction film *Aelita*, directed by Yakov Protazanov in 1924.**

Liubov Popova, photomontage for set of Tretiakov's *The Earth in Turmoil*, 1923.

Two scenes from *The Evening of the* ▲ ▶
Book, Moscow 1924. Costumes
and sets by Stepanova; scripted
and directed by Vitali Zhemchuzny,
Baron Foregger's assistant.

Vsevolod Pudovkin, actor in
Kuleshov's Collective and later film
director in his own right, 1926.
Photo by Dmitri Debabov.

Eccentricism was a logical development from the
alogical thought of the Futurists. Artists introduced
absurd elements or breaks in logic into their work in
order to restructure and reorientate reality. Sergei
Eisenstein used the tricks of circus and music-hall
performers, as well as film to make contemporary
satirical or political points, in Tretiakov's loose
adaptation of Alexander Ostrovsky's *Enough Stupidity in Every Wise Man,* shown at the Moscow Proletkult Theatre in 1923. In Petrograd the Factory of
Eccentric Actors (FEKS) was set up in 1922 by Grigory Kozintsev and Leonid Trauberg; it was also based
on principles derived from vaudeville and the circus.
In their first film, *The Adventures of Oktyabrina*
(1924), the attempts of capitalist lackeys Curzon,
Poincaré and Coolidge to rob a state bank are
thwarted by the intervention of a young pioneer. Lev
Kuleshov's Actors' Collective was at the same time
experimenting with new forms of comedy which had
a strong ideological message. Their first film, *The
Strange Adventures of Mr West in the Land of the
Bolsheviks* (1924), poked fun at American anti-
Soviet stereotypes and was a great popular success.

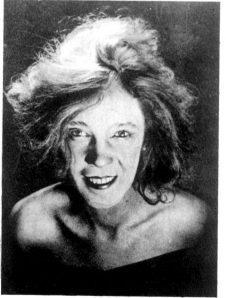

Alexandra Kokhlova, granddaughter
of Pavel Tretiakov and one of the
stars of the Actors' Collective, 1926.

Opening scene from Eisenstein's
production of *Enough Stupidity in
Every Wise Man,* 1923.

Still from *The Adventures of
Oktyabrina,* 1924.

Exhibition of student work exploring space and volume in the foundation department of Vkhutemas, early 1920s.

In 1918 the Moscow Institute of Painting, Sculpture and Architecture and the Stroganov Art School were combined into Svomas (the Free Art Studios). In 1920 these were renamed Vkhutemas (the Higher State Art-Technical Studios) an acronym which was changed to Vkhutein when it became an institute in 1926. In 1930 the experimental, functionalist nature of the organization was negated when it was re-organized as the Moscow Art Institute.

Combining art with design as an essential part of the course, Vkhutemas enlisted the leading avant-garde artists and architects of the 1920s to the ideal of producing 'artist-constructors'.

Rodchenko (second from left) and
students of the Metfak (Metalwork
department) which he ran, 1926.

Life class c. 1923.

El Lissitzky, photomontage
for the architecture department
of Vkhutemas, 1927.

Konstantin Melnikov, 'Makhorka' (Tobacco) Pavilion, 1923.

In the early years after the Revolution building materials were in short supply and many architects worked on utopian projects or temporary structures for exhibitions, where there were fewer practical constraints.

Kasimir Malevich, *Architekton Alpha,* plaster model, 1923.

G. Yakulov and V. Shchuko, Monument to the twenty-six Baku Commissars, 1923. Yakulov is pictured with the model.

V. Shchuko, restaurant and café, both for the All-Russian Agricultural and Handicraft Exhibition, Moscow 1923.

In 1924 Sergei Eisenstein directed *Strike,* his first full-length film. The script had been developed by the Proletkult collective with whom Eisenstein had previously worked as a theatre director. In *Strike* Eisenstein developed his theory of the 'montage of attractions', whereby two opposing images were put together to create a third – a new image both independent of and more intense than its sources. At first Eisenstein's films were more popular abroad than they were in the Soviet Union and his next film, *The Battleship Potemkin* (1925), ran for only two weeks in Moscow whilst it was a huge success in Berlin. Feodor Gladkov's *Cement* (1925) was one of the first Soviet novels to turn away from the conflicts of the Civil War to glorify the heroism of industrial construction. Although criticized by writers during the Cultural Revolution for excessive stylistic ornamentation and gratuitous violence, the novel was extremely popular and provided a model for the Socialist Realist novel of the 1930s. In 1927 *Cement* was made into a film directed by Vladimir Vilner, with sets by Erdman.

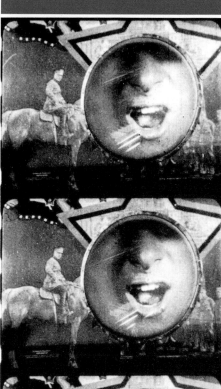

Poster for *Cement*, 1927, by the Stenberg brothers, leading poster designers; it is a striking example of their graphic use of montage.

◀ Stills from *Strike*, 1924.

Stenberg brothers, poster
for Dovzhenko's film *Earth*, 1930.

Gustav Klutsis, 'Women! Train as
Workers', 1927.

Graphic designers and typographers began to work
on a style of communication which would be bold,
easy to read and modern. Fighting against NEP spe-
culation Rodchenko and Mayakovsky worked
together on advertisements for state stores and products. Alexei Gan and Gustav Klutsis worked on posters, leaflets and book covers. Many new Soviet films
were first brought to the attention of the public by the
brightly coloured posters of the Stenberg brothers.

Rodchenko, cover for Mayakovsky's
volume of poems *Syphilis*, 1926.

Georgy Stenberg (*left*) at work with
I. Gerasimovich.

Advertisement hoarding for macaroni
and the Mosselprom store, Moscow,
by Rodchenko and Mayakovsky, 1925.

View of prize-winning display of graphic design by Rodchenko and Mayakovsky in the Grand Palais.

The Soviet pavilions for the 1925 Paris International Exhibition of Decorative Arts were designed to reveal to the West, for the first time, the new forms of Soviet society. Design and industry were planned to serve the material and ideological needs of the people. Beauty, it was argued, was not an end in itself but resulted naturally out of fitness for purpose. Many awards were given to Soviet entries in the Exhibition, particularly Rodchenko and Mayakovsky's advertisements; the new ceramics from the State Porcelain Factory; and the textile designs by young avant-garde artists.

Rodchenko had designed the interior of a workers' club, to be constructed on site, and Isaac Rabinovich had planned a reading room to show off the good design of a wide range of types of book published by Gosizdat, the state publishing house, as their contribution to the concentrated effort to eliminate illiteracy. The new architecture was spectacularly and romantically presented by Konstantin Melnikov's prefabricated wooden pavilion. Melnikov's structure expressed the dynamic, geometric and ideological forms of the Soviet era – forms which, in their lightness, energy and originality, reflected its industrial spirit. The pavilion was a great popular success, so much so that the annual Russian emigré fancy-dress ball in Paris took Melnikov's 'Constructivism' as the theme for that year and invited the architect as a guest of honour.

Interior of Rabinovich's Gosizdat reading room, 1925.

Three views of Melnikov's Soviet pavilion for the 1925 Paris International Exhibition of Decorative Arts. The photo opposite was taken by Rodchenko.

Section for Socialist Development in the planning of the RSFSR, early 1930s.
Left to right standing: G. Savinov, A. Pasternak; *seated:* K. Afanasiev, M. Ginsburg, M. Barsch, N. Sokolov.

Moisei Ginsburg, Gostrakh apartments, 1926-7. Sergei Tretiakov and his family lived in an apartment in this block in central Moscow. Shops were planned at ground level, floors one to three housed model apartments and on the fourth floor was a twelve-roomed communal apartment, above which was a roof garden.

Postcard of the Russakov Factory Club, 1927-8, ▶ designed by Melnikov. Photo by Rodchenko.

Nikolai Maloremov and Victor Andreev, new plan for Zaporozhye in the Ukraine, 1930.

Architects and planners began to consider how the ideals of Communism could be translated into architecture. Workers' clubs which housed sports, health and leisure facilities, and libraries – even in some cases observatories – were built to serve large catchments. Flats with communal facilities were planned. New proposals were drawn up for gigantic cities; some of these were futuristic visions which, following the example of Malevich and Lissitzky, were designed to float in space.

In 1925 the OSA group of architects was founded by Moisei Ginsburg and the Vesnin brothers. Affiliated to the LEF group it was concerned with the problems of communal housing and social planning.

COMMUNAL LIVING

Still from Vertov's thematic documentary *The Man with the Movie Camera*, 1929.

In spite of their good intentions many artists began to find that industries were not willing to accept their designs for production. Then, as now, there was little popular taste for innovation. In the textile industry the influence of the avant-garde did begin to make itself felt in the wide range of thematic designs produced by factory artists but with a few exceptions there was a general reluctance to employ artists from outside.
As a result the avant-garde gravitated increasingly towards the media of graphic design and photography. During 1928 *Novy LEF,* under the editorship of Sergei Tretiakov, became a journal of 'factography'. Photographers, film-makers and writers went into the factories and the countryside to learn about and express the life of the people.

Rodchenko, poster for Vertov's film *Kino Glaz* (Cinema Eye), 1923.

114

Dziga Vertov, film-maker, *c.* 1927.

Sergei Tretiakov, 1927. ▶
Photo by Rodchenko.

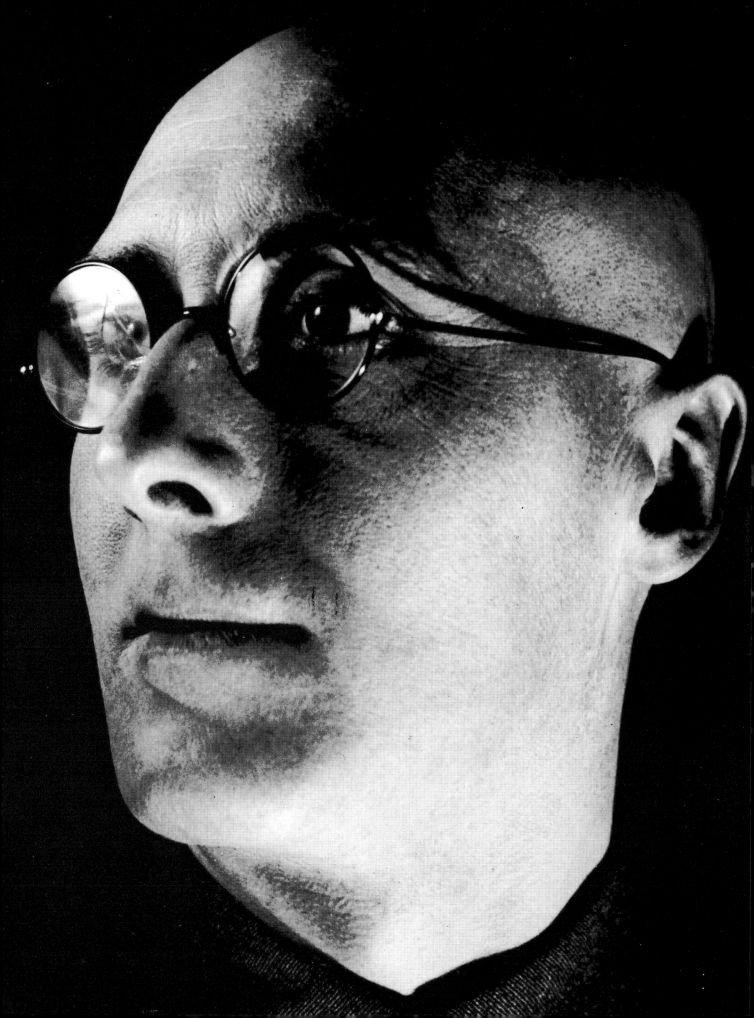

Rodchenko, street scene, 1928.

Rodchenko, telephone, 1927.

Rodchenko, the new Moscow
Planetarium by Barsch and Sinyavsky,
1929.

Boris Ignatovich, restorers reading
an atheist magazine while working on
a church, 1928.

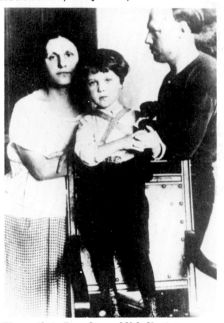

The artists Drevin and Udaltsova
with their son Andrei, 1926.
Photo by Gustav Klutsis.

'Art has no place in modern life. It will continue to
exist . . . only as long as there are people who love
deception and beautiful lies. Every modern cultured
man must wage war against art as against opium.
Photograph and be photographed!'

These extreme words, written by Rodchenko in 1928
in praise of the truth in the ordinary snapshot, did not
spell an end to experimentalism in his work. In many
photographs he adopted unusual viewpoints which
gave previously unsuspected dimensions to ordinary
objects. For this, at the end of the 1920s, he was
accused of 'formalism'. Similar unusual perspectives
were adopted by photographers and film-makers such
as Boris Ignatovich, Lev Kuleshov and Dziga Vertov.

◀ Olga Tretiakova, c. 1928. Photo by Rodchenko.

117

The proletarian movement and the first Five Year Plan

When Lenin died of a stroke in January 1924 there was no obvious successor, but during the following years the Party Secretary, Josef Stalin, managed to outmanoeuvre his rivals until he was virtually in complete control. In 1928 he introduced the first Five Year Plan, a radical programme for the collectivization of agriculture and the development of heavy industry, and society was put more or less on a wartime footing in an uncompromising attempt to catch up with the West and surpass the economic achievements of the United States. All energies, ideological and cultural, had to be subordinated to this aim; dissent became treason.

The revolution in culture paralleled that in the economy. As the growing number of industrial workers provided support for Stalin's policies, so proletarian credentials became essential for advancement. Imports of foreign films and translations of foreign authors were drastically reduced. Both leftist (avantgarde) and rightist (bourgeois intellectual) cultural tendencies were mercilessly denounced by the young party cadres and Komsomols (young Communist League members), who made up the bulk of membership of the proletarian arts organizations. RAPP (the Russian Association of Proletarian Writers), VOPRA (the All Union Association of Proletarian Architects), RAPKh (the Russian Association of Proletarian Artists) and RAPM (the Russian Association of Proletarian Musicians) were encouraged to attack 'formalism' in art. They formed 'raiding parties' of 'light cavalry' which battled to transform every area of society: satire was 'anti-Soviet'; intellectuals were 'class enemies' whose experiments were 'unintelligible to the masses'. This latter charge was levelled by RAPP members at Mayakovsky and he bitterly repudiated it with an exhibition, justifying twenty years of his creative work in a section showing newspaper cuttings of his poems from all over the Union and appreciative notes and letters from workers.

The strident voices of these proletarian groups combined youthful rebellion with the reactionary opinions of the silent majority. The rhetoric they adopted was that of the Civil War: their taste was romantic, idealized and realist: no artist could remain unaffected by the onslaught. By 1932 the consensus was complete and past 'formalists' publicly acknowledged the error of their ways.

The prevailing emphasis, however, on the social origin of work – whether in art or industry – had begun to be counter-productive once the formalists and leftists had been brought to heel and a new, more subtle form of discrimination was found. In April 1932, on the instructions of Stalin, the Central Committee took control of cultural policy by dissolving all the existing proletarian literary and artistic organizations on the grounds that 'they were too narrow and restricted the serious scope of artistic activity'. These were replaced by broadly based Unions which took responsibility for all affairs relating to any one art form. Proletarian culture had been subsumed by Party culture. The Cultural Revolution was complete.

Scene from Nikolai Pogodin's play *My Friend*, with back projection designed by John Heartfield. Theatre of Revolution, Moscow 1932.

From 1928 Kasimir Malevich began to turn his attention away from *Architektons* and *Planits* – Suprematist architectural structures floating in space – towards the concerns of his youth. In 1929 he was to give his last one-man exhibition. The peasant subjects of his paintings of 1911 and 1912 now re-appeared in his work, often embellished with Suprematist ornament. Malevich had combined the primitive 'Russian' quality of his early work with the cosmic universality of Suprematism. This was his final realist utopia.

Malevich, *Farm Woman with a Black Face*, 1928-32.

Malevich, *Woman with a Red Pole*, 1932.

Malevich, *The Red Army*, 1928.

Malevich's body lying in state at the House of the Leningrad Artists' Union, May 1935.
◀ Malevich, *Woman with a Comb*, 1932.

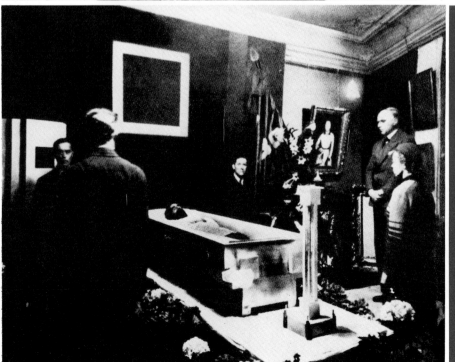

Letatlin on display at the Pushkin Museum of Fine Arts, 1932.

In 1927 Tatlin returned to Moscow from Kiev, where he had been working for a year, to become head of the metalwork, woodwork and ceramics departments of Vkhutein. Two years later he set up a small Experimental Scientific Research Laboratory in one of the towers of the Novodevichy Monastery with students from Vkhutein. His work there was the design and construction according to organic principles of *Letatlin* – a cheaply produced bentwood glider which, he felt, would liberate the society of the future by giving man the ability to soar like a bird. The name of the machine was based on a word-play between his own name and the Russian verb *letat* – to fly.

Like the Monument to the Third International, *Letatlin* was as much a symbol of a new vision as a practical project. Prior to its flight trials outside Moscow in 1933 its structure, development drawings and finished form were exhibited at the Pushkin Museum of Fine Arts in Moscow and at the Russian Museum in Leningrad.

Tatlin's laboratory was disbanded in 1932 along with all other literary and artistic organizations.

Novodevichy Monastery.
◀ Test-flying *Letatlin* outside Moscow, 1933.

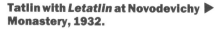

Letatlin with Tatlin in the pilot's position, c. 1932.

Tatlin with *Letatlin* at Novodevichy ▶ Monastery, 1932.

LEARNING TO FLY

фото А.ТЕМЕРИН.

During the late 1920s Meyerhold's theatre underwent a crisis in finding new avant-garde plays to add to the repertoire. Reacting against the worthiness and false heroism of much self-consciously 'proletarian' culture, the leftist avant-garde produced satires, which were often transposed to the world of the future. Mayakovsky's two plays, *The Bedbug* (1928) with incidental music by the young Dmitri Shostakovich, and *The Bath-house* (1930) both castigated contemporary petit-bourgeois bad taste and mindless bureaucracy. *The Bath-house* in particular was heavily criticized by RAPP, which held that art should only depict 'real life' and that any satire was essentially anti-socialist. This opposition delayed the public performance of the play for nearly four years; even when it did appear in March 1930, it was in an atmosphere of hostility and nearly every press review was destructive. Mayakovsky and Meyerhold fought back, incorporating rhyming slogans ridiculing the censor, RAPP critics and the Moscow Arts Theatre. But the production was not a popular success and was soon dropped from the repertoire.

Yuri German's *Prelude* (1932-3) was the last work by a Soviet writer to be shown publicly at the Meyerhold Theatre. Facing increasing criticism from the Press and the Party, Meyerhold henceforth sought refuge in a classical repertoire.

Cyrogenics in the year 1979: Prisypkin being unfrozen. From the second part of Mayakovsky's *The Bedbug*, 1928, at the Meyerhold Theatre. Sets and costumes by Rodchenko. Photo by A. Temerin.

'The Restaurant' – the second act of Yuri German's play *Prelude*, staged by Meyerhold in 1932-3.

Caricature of *The Bath-house*, 1928, by the Kukriniksy. Mayakovsky is in the bath having his toenails cut by Lunacharsky; other prominent bathers are Pushkin, Gorky and Alexei Tostoy.

Mayakovsky's *The Bath-house*, 1930. ▶
Directed by Meyerhold;
sets by Vakhtangov and Deineka.

A late example of Constructivist set design by the Stenberg brothers for *The Line of Fire* by Nikolai Nikitin at Tairov's Kamerny Theatre, Moscow 1931.

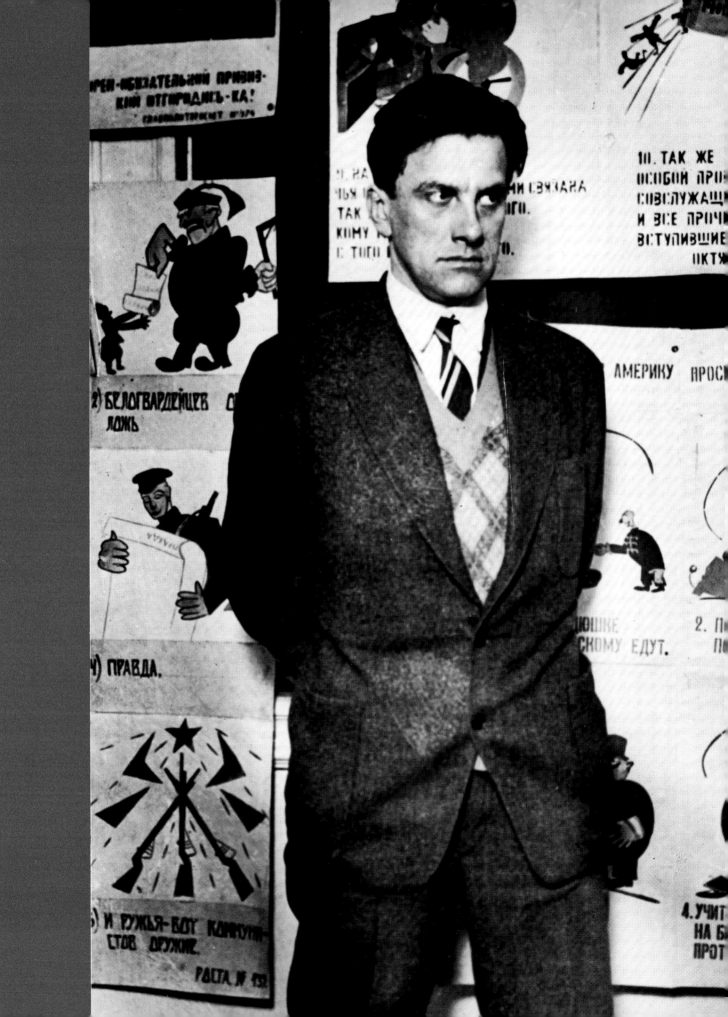

Funeral procession.

Vladimir Mayakovsky, 1924. Photo by Rodchenko.

On 14 April 1930, at the age of 36, Mayakovsky shot himself. Red catafalque for Mayakovsky's coffin, designed by Tatlin and the students of Vkhutein.

Mayakovsky lying in state at the House of Writers, Moscow. *Centre:* Osip Brik; *right:* Lily Brik and Mayakovsky's mother.

◀ Mayakovsky at the opening of his exhibition Twenty Years of Work at the Moscow House of Writers, 1930.

**Watersports — a postcard by
Gustav Klutsis for the Spartakiada
Games, Moscow 1928.**

**Morning exercises, 1935.
Photo by Rodchenko.**

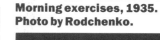

**Sports parade in Red Square, 1932.
Photo by Georgy Zelma.**

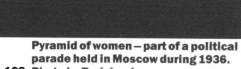

**Pyramid of women — part of a political
parade held in Moscow during 1936.
Photo by Rodchenko.**

Just as the promotion of literacy and education were high priorities for the new proletarian society, so was the encouragement of physical fitness. The new man and woman of the Soviet future would inevitably be healthier and quicker than in the past: the body as much as the mind had to be trained to peak efficiency. Sport became the mass culture of the 1920s and 30s and was encouraged at every level, as it promoted fitness and teamwork.

Human wheel – part of a parade held in Red Square, Moscow 1936.

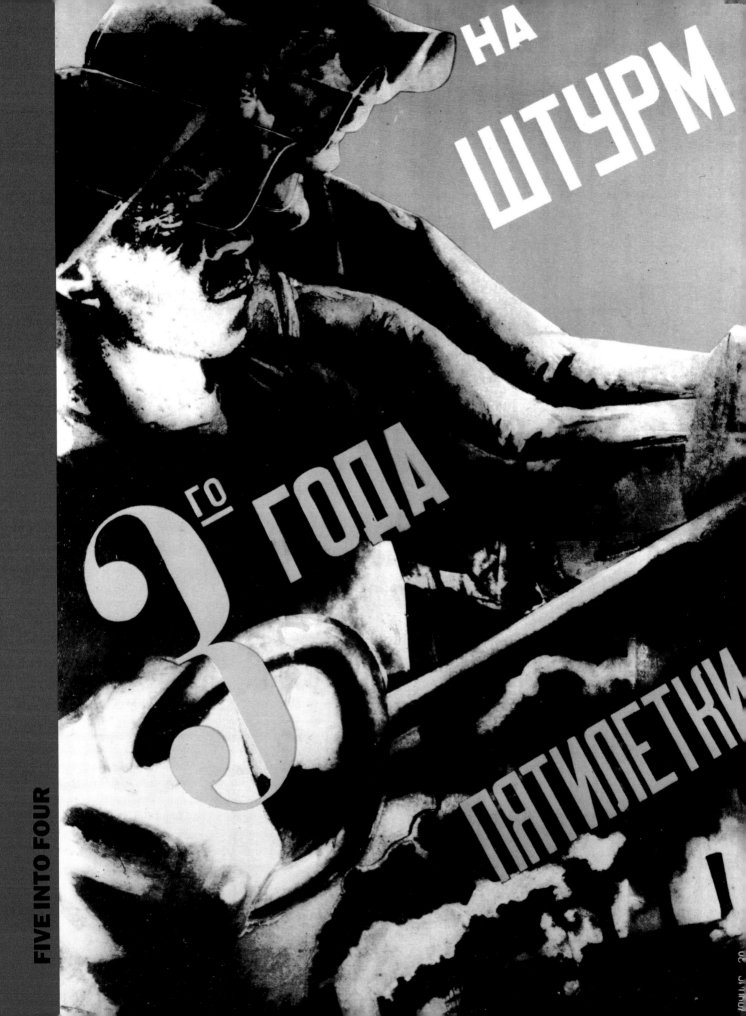

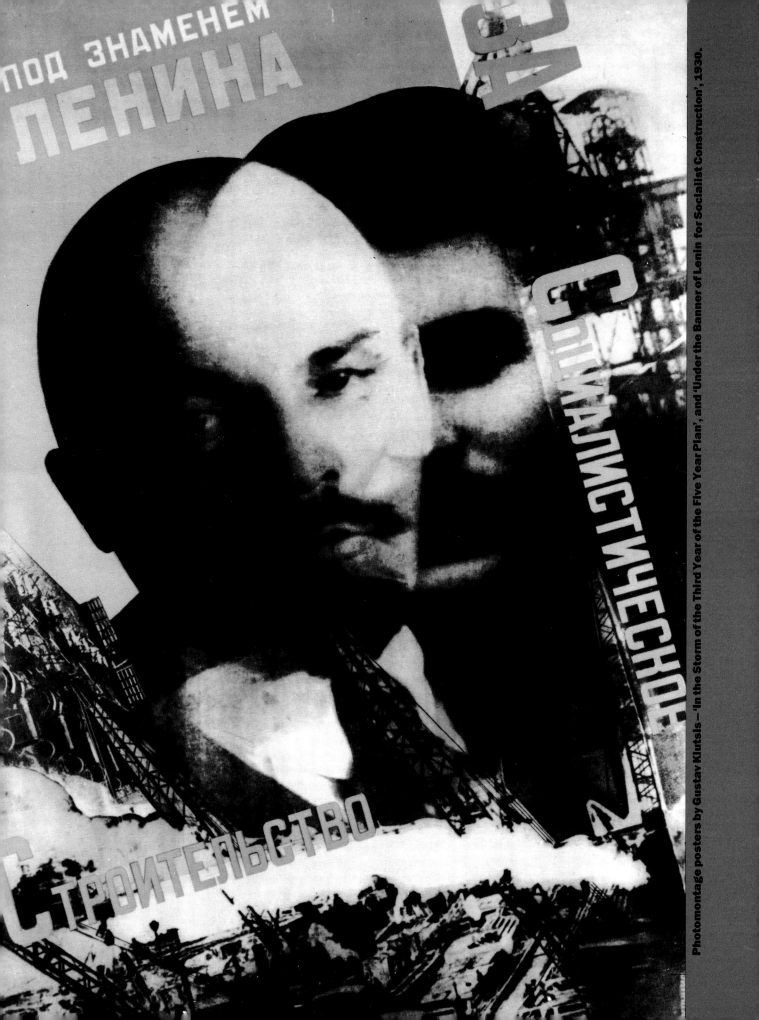

ПОД ЗНАМЕНЕМ
ЛЕНИНА

СОЦИАЛИСТИЧЕСКОЕ

СТРОИТЕЛЬСТВО

Two non-heroic views of the newly built industrial city of Magnitogorsk, in the Ural mountains, taken during Margaret Bourke-White's photojournalistic assignment in the Soviet Union, 1930-1. Working conditions were appalling and children were enlisted onto the building sites

MAGNITOGORSK

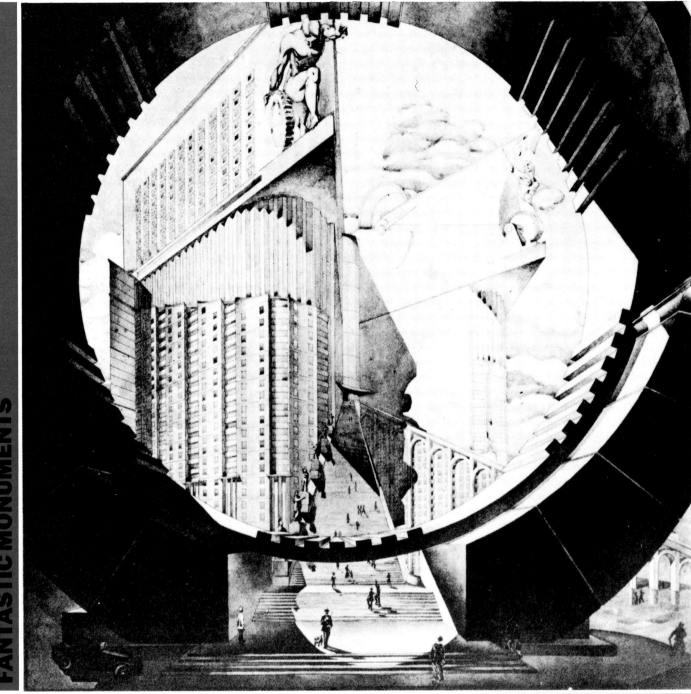

Architects also responded to the heroic call for new monumental forms. Melnikov's submission to the competition for the Commissariat of Heavy Industry (Narkomtiazprom), in 1934, is based on a repetition of the Roman numeral V representing the five years of the Five Year Plans. This motif is repeated in the elevation where, viewed through a portal, a grand stairway rises to a large plaza. The Commissariat was part of a grandiose new plan for Moscow which was never built, and would have been sited in the Red Square facing Lenin's tomb; this would have necessitated the demolition of the State Historical Museum.

From 1925 Iakov Chernikov, 'the Soviet Piranesi', had set up in Leningrad his own research and ex-

perimental laboratory to look at architectural forms and methods of graphic representation. Here, with the help of a trained team of draughtsmen, he produced a series of books showing fantastic forms; these ranged from Suprematist-influenced axonometrics to futuristic renditions of industrial complexes and cities, to the classical perfection of Palaces of Communism.

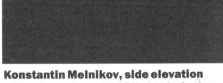

Konstantin Melnikov, side elevation of the Commissariat of Heavy Industry, 1934, and view through portal.

Iakov Chernikov, an axonometric representation of a factory building, 1933.

Two stills from *The Old and the New*, 1929.

Inauguration of the Turksib Railway, 1929.

Poster by Gustav Klutsis
on the provision of transport, 1929.

The first Five Year Plan confronted the problems of building heavy industries and power plants and the collectivization of peasant agriculture. Both tasks were formidable and were achieved at great cost. Collectivization in particular met much opposition from entrenched peasant farmers who would spoil their crops or slaughter livestock rather than hand them over. In March 1930 in an article in *Pravda* entitled 'Dizzy with Success', Stalin tried to blame the 'excesses' of collectivization on the fervour of local party workers. However the policy and resistance to it continued until, by the following year, the *Kolkhoz* or collective farm was firmly entrenched in the Soviet countryside.

Eisenstein's film *The Old and the New* (1929) took as its subject the collectivization of the countryside, showing the revolutionary effect of the tractor on peasant agriculture and using a new model farm designed by Andrei Burov, one of the leading Soviet disciples of Le Corbusier.

Communications were vital to the establishment of industry and the opening of the Turkestan-Siberia (Turksib) Railway became an important achievement of the first Five Year Plan.

138 Kuzma Petrov-Vodkin, *The Alarm, The Year 1919,* **1934-5.**

V. Perelman, *Literature Circle at the Amo Works*, 1932.

The proletarian groups favoured realism in art as it could be used to reinforce the values of the Soviet state. Alexander Gerasimov's *Lenin on the Tribune* (1930) is a romantic view of Lenin's oratory by Stalin's favourite artist. Artists and writers were encouraged to go out to work in factories or with brigades on construction sites and to record what they saw. V. Perelman's *Literature Circle at the Amo Works* (1932) shows one aspect of cultural activities in a vast Moscow factory. Kuzma Petrov-Vodkin's painting *The Alarm* (1934-5) refers to the time of White atrocities during the Civil War, while the stillness of Solomon Nikritin's *People's Court* (1933) is more redolent of *The Last Supper* than the punitive judicial procedures of the Stalin era. Maligned in the West because of its allegedly Stalinist associations, the Soviet realist painting of the 1920s and 1930s still awaits reassessment.

Solomon Nikritin, *People's Court*, 1933.

Alexander Gerasimov,
***Lenin on the Tribune*, 1930.**

ДНЕПРОСТРОЙ СТАНЕТ [...] ПАМЯТЬЮ ПЕРВОГО ЭЛЕКТРО-ФИКАТОРА в С.С.С.Р. В.И. ЛЕНИНА.

◀ **Photomontage by El Lissitzky, 'Dnieprostroi will be the great monument of the electrification of the USSR, V. I. Lenin', from *USSR in Construction* No. 10, 1932.**

The monthly magazine *USSR in Construction*, printed in Russian and three foreign languages between 1930 and 1941, chronicled the achievements of the Five Year Plans and spared no expense in its innovatory layouts and high-quality photogravure. A number of leading avant-garde artists, including El Lissitzky, Rodchenko and Stepanova, designed special issues, in some cases contributing photographs they had taken themselves.

The new hydro-electric power station on the Dnieper River, 1934. Photo by Georgy Petrusov.

'All of Moscow is building the Metro' proclaims Gustav Klutsis's 1934 poster. Lazar Kaganovich, Moscow City boss and architect of the scheme, looks on.

Tea service by the Lomonosov Porcelain Factory, Leningrad, commemorating the opening of the Moscow Metro, 1937.

Kievskaya Station on the underground ▶ railway in Moscow, opened in 1937. The fine marble and the decorated colonnades re-created the opulence of the old régime for the workers' state.

Part of Stalin's new scheme for Moscow under the first Five Year Plan was the placing of the Kremlin on the central axis between two huge buildings – the Palace of the Soviets and the Commissariat of Heavy Industry (*see* p. 134). The scale of each was so grandiose that neither progressed beyond foundation level. The competition for the Palace of the Soviets was opened in 1931 and plans were to take into account the 110,000-square-metre site, which occupied the territory of the demolished Cathedral of the Redeemer – a monument to the victory of 1812. Over 160 designs were submitted, including many from leading international architects. In the summer of 1933 the Commission of Adjudication, under Molotov, announced that there was no outright winner, but that the design by the Russian architect Boris Iofan should be used as a working basis for the palace and that fellow architects Shchuko and Gelfreikh should help him revise the plans. The main clause stipulated by the Commission concerned the 18-metre-high statue of a 'liberated proletarian' which surmounted the building; this was to be substituted by a 75-metre-high statue of Lenin. It was intended that building would start by 1 July 1935, but it was not until 1937 that the revised plans were accepted. At 435 metres high, the palace was to be the largest building in the world – surpassing the Empire State Building and the Eiffel Tower. It was to contain two large halls to seat 20,000 and 8000 people, which would accommodate meetings of the Supreme Soviet and Party Congresses. Offices, restaurants and other amenities were also planned. During the War the unfinished steel framework of the building was dismantled to provide materials for the war effort; the project was never subsequently revived and the site now hosts a large open-air swimming pool.

Boris Iofan, design for the Palace of the Soviets, 1933.

THE STEEL COLOSSUS

Revolutionary romanticism and the cult of Stalin

During the second Five Year Plan (1933-7) Stalin dispensed with the help of the existing young proletarian groups which had swept away the last vestiges of NEP attitudes, and began to manipulate history on a much grander scale. As he strengthened his grip on the Party many superlatives were used of him in the Press: 'the Steel Colossus', one of the less effusive descriptions, reflects clearly the mood of monumental heroism which typified the time.

In 1934 two crucial events took place: in August, at the First All-Union Congress of Soviet Writers, Andrei Zhdanov called for the portrayal of life 'in its revolutionary development'. The new Soviet artist should 'break with the old-style romanticism that depicted a non-existent life with non-existent heroes, which spirited the reader away from the contradictions and oppression of life to an unreal world, to a world of utopias.' Such became the doctrinal base of Socialist Realism which, in literature and throughout the arts, amounted to little more than the subordination of creativity to the dictates of the Party.

The second event, in December, was the assassination of Sergei Kirov, the Leningrad Party boss and political rival to Stalin. Engineered by Stalin, this provided the pretext for a widening series of purges and show trials which was to decimate the intelligentsia and even the upper echelons of the Party itself. Of the members of the Central Committee at the 1934 Seventeenth Party Congress (the 'Congress of Victors'), 70 per cent were to be executed for subversion during the next five years. Stalin used the purges ruthlessly to strengthen his own power, and the government of the country became increasingly synonymous with his will.

The forms and materials of Socialist Realism were heroic, heavy and monumental, and reflected the prevailing current of 'revolutionary romanticism'. Artists were described by Stalin himself as 'engineers of the human soul' and as such were entrusted, along with all other workers, with the task of bringing about the materialistic millennium. Painting in this style had to be realist and, like the work of the nineteenth-century Wanderers, illustrative of a theme. Design and architecture were to be imposing rather than functional, and expressive of the power of the working people. Stalin felt that the new Soviet man and woman were as worthy of palaces as the pre-Revolutionary aristocracy had been, and that is what he built for them.

It could be argued that such an aggressive, highly focused art was wholly in keeping with the demands of a planned economy and with the steadily increasing international tension of the 1930s. Yet Socialist Realism and the values it embodied were not purely the results of the expedient policies of Stalin and his followers but, as we have seen, came out of a long and steady evolution of political, social and aesthetic theory which had developed from the middle of the last century. It was for this reason that Socialist Realism was so widely, and in some cases enthusiastically, accepted – it had grown organically out of the soil of established Russian culture and gave a voice to people who felt that they had remained silent for too long.

Statue in honour of Stalin's rival, Sergei Kirov, erected in Baku, Azerbaijan, c. 1933.

1935 poster by Gustav Klutsis showing Stalin and Voroshilov, head of the Armed Forces. The slogan reads: 'Long Live the Red Workers' and Peasants' Army, Loyal Guardians of the Soviet Frontiers.'

ДА ЗДРАВСТВУЕТ РАБОЧЕ-КРЕСТЬЯНСКАЯ КРАСНАЯ АРМИ
ВЕРНЫЙ СТРАЖ СОВЕТСКИХ ГРАНИЦ

..ЦЕЛЬЮ СОЮЗА ЯВЛЯЮТСЯ: СВЕРЖЕНИЕ БУРЖУАЗИИ, ГОСПОДСТВО ПРОЛЕТАРИАТА, УНИЧТОЖЕНИЕ СТАРОГО, ПОКОЯЩЕГОСЯ НА КЛАССОВЫХ ПРОТИВОПОЛОЖНОСТЯХ БУРЖУАЗНОГО ОБЩЕСТВА, И СОЗДАНИЕ НОВОГО ОБЩЕСТВА БЕЗ КЛАССОВ И ЧАСТНОЙ СОБСТВЕННОСТИ". К.МАРКС

MILITANT SOCIALISM

Poster by Gustav Klutsis to commemorate the fiftieth anniversary of the death of Karl Marx, 1933. Klutsis designed a number of posters in the early 1930s which promoted the cause of world Communism.

МЫ СТОИМ ЗА МИР ОТСТАИВАЕМ ДЕЛО МИ НО МЫ НЕ БОИМС УГРОЗ И ГОТОВЫ ОТВЕТИ УДАРОМ НА УДА ПОДЖИГАТЕЛЕЙ ВОЙН И.СТАЛ

Anti-fascist poster by Gustav Klutsis in 1934 bearing Stalin's words: 'We stand for peace and struggle for peace but we fear no threat and are ready to answer aggressors blow for blow.'

PARIS 1937

The dynamic lines of Boris Iofan's Soviet pavilion for the 1937 Paris World Exhibition were rooted in the Trocadero Gardens. Over the stepped, almost Art Deco tower which dominated the central entrance a vast, specially commissioned sculpture, *The Worker and the Collective Farm Girl* by Vera Mukhina, rose triumphant. This heroic representation of a couple striding forward, their arms raised and clasped in a salute, symbolized the alliance of industry and agriculture which was at the root of the Five Year Plans.

Vera Mukhina, *The Worker and the Collective Farm Girl*, 1937.

The engineer, industrial worker and collectivized peasant were the heroes of the Five Year Plans. The super-heroes were called Stakhanovites after Alexei Grigorevich Stakhanov, a coal miner who surpassed all previous records of production. Alexander Deineka was specially commissioned to produce a large decorative panel for Boris Iofan's 1937 Paris pavilion, showing the Moscow of the future: the new Soviet men, women and children confidently marching ahead — the Kremlin on their left, the as yet unbuilt Palace of the Soviets behind them. Nikolai Suetin, a former pupil of Malevich who subsequently became chief artist at the Lomonosov State Porcelain Factory, designed the interiors of the pavilion. The fluted planes of the columns and the geometric lines of the vases echo memories of Suprematism. Iofan's model for the Palace of the Soviets is placed decisively at the head of the main stair.

Foyer of the Soviet pavilion at the 1937 Paris exhibition.

Alexander Deineka, 'The Stakhanovites', sketch for a panel for the 1937 International Exhibition, Paris.

Suetin's design for the interiors of the Paris pavilion, with Iofan's model for the Palace of the Soviets at the head of the main stair.

Statue of Lenin in the Soviet pavilion.

Mikhail Bulgakov

Isaac Babel

With Stalin at the helm formalism, non-conformism and unpredictable creativity were immediately and virulently denounced. Many artists disappeared, victims of the purges and the secret police; others managed to survive either by distancing themselves from an 'unreliable' past or by affirming their support of the present. Some followed Isaac Babel's advice and observed 'the genre of silence' but this alone was not enough to guarantee safety. These artists are now officially rehabilitated within the Soviet Union but it is still not possible to gain access to all of their works.

Evgeny Zamyatin

Osip Mandelstam

Vsevolod Meyerhold ▶

THANKING THE LEADER

'Comrade Germanyuk, member of
the Plenipotentiary Commission
of the National Assembly of Western
Byelorussia, thanks Stalin for
the liberation of the people from
the Polish yoke, 1939.'

PICTURE CREDITS

Illustrations are identified by page number and, where necessary, т=top, в=bottom, c=centre, ʟ=left, ʀ=right.

Museums and Galleries

AMSTERDAM, Gemeente Museum 60 вʀ; Stedelijk Museum 59 вʀ, 60 тʟ. COLOGNE, Galerie Gmurzynska 17 т, 17 вʟ, 65, 71 тʀ, 75 тʟ, 131, 142 ʟ, 148-9. KALININ, Art Gallery 152-3 в. KOSTROMA, Museum of Fine Art 59 тʟ. LENINGRAD, Brodsky Museum 49 вʟ; Museum of Revolution 48; Russian Museum 17 вʀ, 24 тʀ, 40 ʀ, 49 вʀ, 51 вʀ, 90, 121 ʟ, 138, 139 вʟ. LONDON, Arts Council 21 т, 58, 59 тʀ, 72 в, 76 ʀ, 77, 138; Fischer Fine Art Ltd 130; Victoria and Albert Museum 9. MOSCOW, Glinka Museum 30 вʀ; Rodchenko Archive 82 вʀ, 83 ʟ, 92 тʀ, 110 тʀ; State Mayakovsky Museum 126, 127 т, 127 вʀ, 127 вʟ; Tretiakov Gallery 11 вʀ, 11 ʀ, 24 вʀ, 30 т, 38, 39 т, 41, 50 в, 51 т, 53 в, 80 т*, 88 т, 89 вʟ*, 89 т*, 120, 121 тʀ, 139 вʀ*, 139 ʀ. NEW YORK, Museum of Modern Art 17 тʀ; Syracuse University 132, 133. ONTARIO, Art Gallery 78 т. OXFORD, Ashmolean 10; Museum of Modern Art 12 вʟ, 13 ʀ, 16 cʟ, 16 тʟ, 20 ʀ, 22 т, 80 ʟ, 80 вʀ, 83 ʟ, 83 тʀ, 92 тʟ, 93 тʀ, 94, 95 тʀ, 95 вʀ, 95 вʟ, 100 тʟ, 100 тʀ, 100 тc, 101, 103 тʀ, 104, 107, 108 вc, 114 вʀ, 115, 116, 124 т, 127 тʟ, 128 тʟ, 128 cʀ, 128 тʀ, 129. STUTTGART, Staatsgalerie 61. TBILISI, Art Gallery 59 вʟ. *Gift of George Costakis, 1977.

Individuals and Agencies

BBC Hulton Picture Library 64 cʟ; Robert Chenciner 88 в; Catherine Cooke 57 в; © 1981 George Costakis. The George Costakis Collection (Owned by Art. Co. Ltd.) 12 т, 24 ʟ, 50 т, 51 вʟ, 99 вʀ; David King Collection 47, 68-9, 135, 140, 156-7; M. Lyons 32; Mansell Collection 55 вʟ; Gordon McVay 91 вʟ, 91 cʀ; National Film Archive 25 тc, 73 c, 98, 99 тʀ, 100 вc, 106 вʀ, 106 тc, 136; Novosti Press Agency 72 т, 76, 137 т; Private collections 79 вʀ, 81; Ilia Rudiak 154 т; Society for Cultural Relations with the USSR 22 в, 76 ʟ, 85, 96, 97 тʀ, 124, 125 вʟ, 143 ʀ, 147; Sygma 67, 71 вʀ; Roger-Viollet 34, 35 т, 35 вʟ, 110 cʀ, 110 вʀ, 127 вʀ, 150, 151.

BIBLIOGRAPHY

Artists' Texts

Bann, S., ed. *The Tradition of Constructivism*, London 1974.
Bowlt, J. E., ed. *Russian Art of the Avant-garde: Theory and Criticism 1902-1934*, New York 1976.
Gassner, H. and Gillen, E. *Zwischen Revolutionskunst und Sozialistischen Realismus. Dokumente und Kommentäre, Kunstdebaten in der Sowjetunion von 1917 bis 1934*, Cologne 1979.
Art et poésie russes 1900-1932, Textes choisis, Centre Georges Pompidou, Paris 1979.

Catalogues

Art into Production: Soviet Ceramics, Textiles and Fashion 1917-1935, Museum of Modern Art, Oxford 1984.
Art in Revolution, Seibu Art Museum, Tokyo 1984.
Barron, S. and Tuchman, M., eds. *The Avant-garde in Russia 1910-1930*, Los Angeles County Museum of Art, 1980.
From Painting to Design. Russian Constructivist Art of the Twenties, Galerie Gmurzynska, Cologne 1981.
Kunst in die Produktion! 1927-32, Berlin, Neue Gesellschaft für Bildende Kunst, 1977.
Paris-Moscou 1900-1930, Centre Georges Pompidou, Paris 1979.
The Suprematist Straight Line, Annely Juda Fine Art, London 1977.
Women Artists of the Russian Avant-garde, Galerie Gmurzynska, Cologne 1979.

Books

Andreeva, L. *Sovetsky Sarfor 1920-30*, Moscow 1975.
Baburina, Nina *The Soviet Political Poster*, Harmondsworth 1985.
Bojko, Szymon *New Graphic Design in Revolutionary Russia*, New York 1972.
Bowlt, J. E. *The Silver Age: Russian Art of the early twentieth century, the World of Art Group*, Newtonville 1979.
Braun, Edward *The Theatre of Meyerhold*, London 1979.
Christie, I. and Gillett, J., eds. *Futurism, Formalism, Feks, Eccentrism and Soviet Cinema 1918-1936*, London (BFI) 1978.
Compton, S. *The World Backwards: Russian Futurist Books 1912-16*, London 1978.
Cooke, C., ed. *Russian Avant-garde art and Architecture*, London 1983.
Fedotova, A. *Paintings of the First Five Year Plan period*, Leningrad 1981.
Fülop-Miller, R. *The Mind and Face of Bolshevism. An examination of cultural life in the Soviet Union*, London 1927.
Gray, C. *The Great Experiment. Russian Art 1863-1922*, London 1962, Rev. edn. under the title *The Russian Experiment in Art 1863-1922*, 1986.
Guerman, M. *Art of the October Revolution*, New York 1979.
Khan-Magomedov, S. O. *Pioniere der Sowjetischen Architektur*, Vienna-Berlin 1983, London 1987.
Lebedev, A. *The Itinerants. Russian Realist artists of the late 19th and early 20th centuries*, Leningrad 1977.
Leyda, J. *Kino, A History of the Russian and Soviet Film*, London 1960.
Lodder, C. *Russian Constructivism*, Newhaven, Conn. 1983.
Milner, J. *Vladimir Tatlin and the Russian Avant-garde*, Newhaven, Conn. 1983.
Nakov, A. B. *L'Avant-garde russe*, Paris 1984, London 1986.
Porter, C. and King, D. *Blood and Laughter, Caricatures from the 1905 Revolution*, London 1985.
Rudenstine, A. *Russian Avant-garde Art: The George Costakis Collection*, London 1981.
Shudakov, Grigory; Suslova, Olga; and Ukhtomskaya, Lilya *Pioneers of Soviet Photography*, London 1983.
Slonim, M. *Russian Theatre from the Empire to the Soviets*, Cleveland 1961.
Starr, S. Frederick *Melnikov: Solo Architect in a Mass Society*, Princeton 1978.
Zhadova, I. *Malevich, Suprematism and Revolution in Russian Art*, London 1982.
Zsadova, Larisza, ed. *Tatlin*, Budapest 1985, London 1987.

INDEX

Page numbers in italic refer to pictures